Realms *of* Light

*Clairvoyant Experiences
of Life After Death*

Laurie Conrad

Design & Ornament
Diana Souza

In gratitude to all Divine Beings

BOOK DESIGN & ILLUSTRATION
Diana Souza

ART TEMPLE
www.art-temple.com

AUTHOR
Laurie Conrad

FIGARO BOOKS
www.figarobooks.com

ABOUT THE COVER

Cover photo illustration & design: Diana Souza
Cover photo: Louise McConnell (L) and Laurie Conrad (R)
Manasquan, New Jersey in the mid-1980's.
Photo: Glenn Williams

NOTE FROM THE AUTHOR

Some of the names in this book have been changed, and in some cases identifying features and places have been altered to protect identities. However, my clairvoyant experiences and dreams and those of others have not been altered in any way, save for the above changes of name and occasionally place. The interviews were taken down verbatim, and remain unchanged as well.

AuthorHouse™
1663 Liberty Drive, Suite 200
Bloomington, IN 47403
www.authorhouse.com
Phone: 1-800-839-8640

First published by AuthorHouse 01/28/2008

ISBN: 978-1-4343-6308-4 (sc)
ISBN: 978-1-4343-6309-1 (e)

Printed in the United States of America
Bloomington, Indiana

This book is printed on acid-free paper.

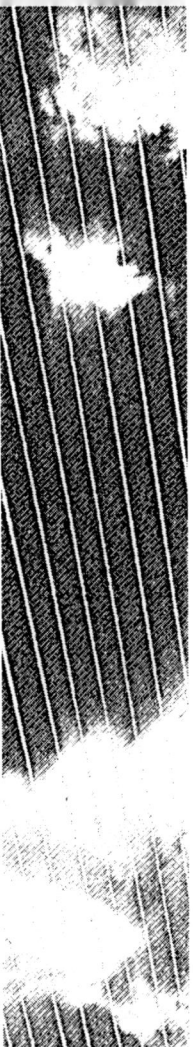

I would like to thank Paul Brunton's son
Kenneth Thurston Hurst
for encouraging me to write books
about my mystical experiences.

SECTION II:

Visits with my Animal Friends in Other Realms

SECTION III: *Interviews with Others*

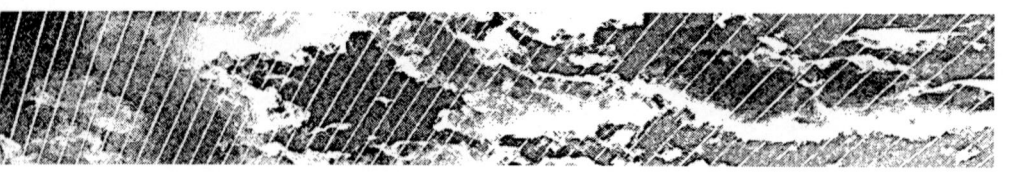

TABLE OF CONTENTS

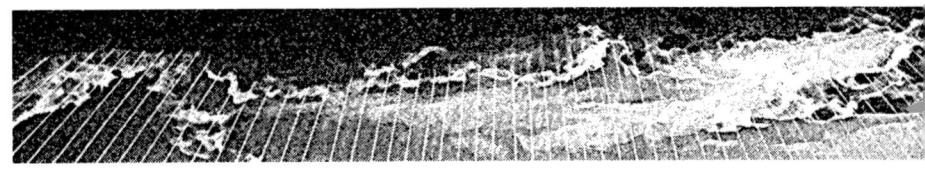

SECTION IV: *Photos*

SECTION V: *Postludes*

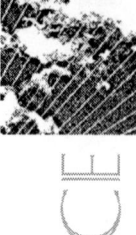

*The intent of this book is to speak of other realms and my
experiences as a clairvoyant in other realms. And many of
those realms are infinitely Beautiful and filled with Love
and Light.*

However, had this volume been of a different nature, I could
have written endless poetry about my friends here on earth.
A page on Eleanor's eyes, another page on the timbre of her
voice – the way she walked or sat, the structure of her sentences and the various patterns and inflections of her mind.
How her clothes moved as she walked, and folded as she sat.
The sounds and rhythms and pitches of her shoes on my living room floor, or out in the gardens, or on the cement and
asphalt paths we followed into town. The touch and outline
of her hand as she opened the front door or held a book.
The inner life that manifested, radiated in a myriad of ways,
in the countless words and expressions and regards, movements and sounds that we shared in all the years we knew
each other on earth.

All my friends, any person I have ever seen or met or read of
– whether it be for a fleeting instant on the street, or a photograph, or in a book or dream, or in my life – all have a
uniqueness that cannot be duplicated, not even in part, not
in a single glance or touch or word.

This I cannot capture for you in these stories. You yourself
will have to imagine what time and space will not allow.

The Journey

From realm to realm,

we follow and find each other

and we will always know each other

by our Light and by our Love.

There is no Death, no end.

As God IS

so we, His frail emissaries

of Divinity and Light here on Earth —

also ARE, eternally.

For the soul is eternal and immortal.

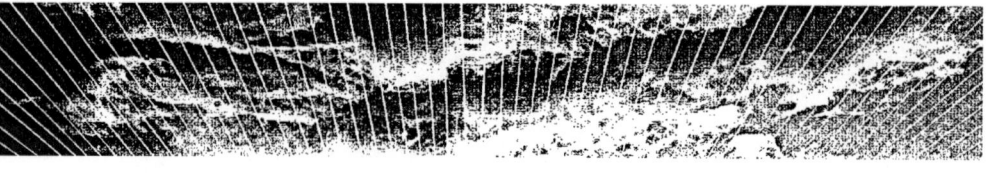

In my work with the Distant Healing Network, I receive many healing requests for the pain and sorrow experienced after the death of a loved one.

One of my healees, who later became my friend, suggested that I write this volume. She was struggling to recover from the death of her father, and we sent many e-mails back and forth. In one e-mail she wrote that many people would want to know what I clairvoyantly experienced of other realms and the souls in those realms. After a few helpful communications on the topic of writing such a book, she sent me the following e-mail in the early fall of 2002:

Hi hon,

A friend of mine lost her Mom last year, and she just wanted to know for sure that there was an afterlife, that her Mom wasn't just a lump in the ground now.

That's what we all really want to know with certainty, that they are happy and OK. That death isn't just the end. That we don't die without it being our own time, that we don't need to feel guilty because we think we should have done more in the hospital to save them. You could explain the whole process, where they are, what they are doing. How do we increase the chances of personal contact, personal contact where there can be no question in our minds that it is real. What are some prayers to say for our loved ones. What are some signs we overlook or rationalize away. Tell people what you see.

xoxox Linda

Basically, I have taken Linda's e-mail as the outline for this book. This volume is not a textbook on life after death. Rather, it is a volume of my clairvoyant experiences of souls in other realms, and the experiences and perceptions of others I have interviewed. I do not pretend to know and understand all the Mysteries of the universe. I am also not a Bible scholar nor a

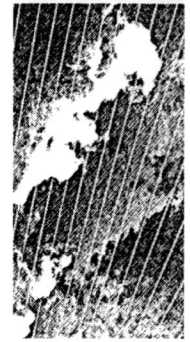

theologian, but only a clairvoyant. The Mysteries of Life and the Soul are vast, no human will ever understand them all. At most, I can only attempt to describe the Glimpses of other realms given to me over the course of my own life, and record the experiences of others.

Some of these perceptions of beings in or from other realms, and the realms they are in, were experienced clairvoyantly in waking state consciousness, others in dream state. I hope that my experiences and the experiences of others in this book will help many to better understand the ways in which we can and do communicate with those we love in other realms – whether we are clairvoyant or not.

I was fortunate to find many willing friends who agreed to be interviewed for this book. In typing up their interviews I was struck by how we all struggle to find words, find a vocabulary for our experiences. For what we perceive in these other realms is very different from our ordinary life and perceptions here on earth. I also noticed that in almost all the accounts, at some point in the interview the persons being interviewed slipped into the present tense when describing their experiences of other realms – even if the rest of the interview is in the past tense. I think this is because those experiences are so deeply felt, so impressed on our minds, that they seem timeless, eternal in a way. And in describing them, we are once again brought into that timeless place that always IS. You could also say that those experiences are given to us in a different consciousness, and to recall them we must return to that consciousness. I will leave this analysis to the philosophers and theologians, to those who have a deeper understanding and training than I.

ONE FINAL COMMENT

I put the word "died" in quotation marks throughout this book, because we clairvoyants can tell you that no one ever "dies." No matter what realm we are in – we are still quite alive.

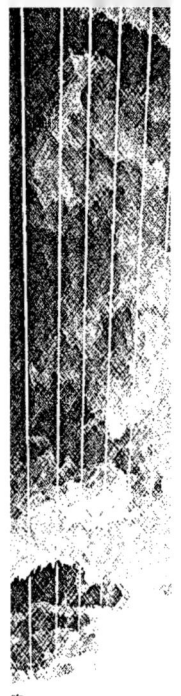

My Experiences in Other Realms

Although I had often seen angels as a child, and looked into other realms – my first conscious visit to another realm was to be with my father. I was still in college when he "died," and not at all ready to say goodbye to him permanently.

Nonetheless, he left for other realms one night, and I felt abandoned and very alone. It was a dark and scary time for me. I remember standing alone by Quarry Bridge one cold, windy autumn evening and looking up at the moon, feeling a hundred or so years old. And then I had the Dream.

I had always dreamt in black and white – or worse, in shades of grey. This dream, however, was in vivid colours – deep, rich, vibrant hues, and not the shades of colour we usually see on Earth. And I have never forgotten the dream, nor the colours. I can step into it whenever I wish.

I had come to see my father, and he was outside mowing the back lawn of a house I had never before been in – and the grass was a deep green of an unusual colour, almost startling in its intensity. It was a sunny, bright day. The sun was a true yellow, like a crayon drawing of the sun, and in the wrong place in the sky for that time of day. Even in my "dream," I knew that I was not on Earth because of the position of the sun. After a while my father finished mowing and we both went into the house. My father sat down in a big, stuffed armchair of a light beige colour, and smiled at me. He was young again, youthful and healthy and trim, with blond hair and piercing blue eyes. When I knew him he had dark black hair – but as a younger man in his twenties, he had been blond.

He smiled at me in a radiant way – his entire being was radiant – and we spoke together for a time about various things that I do not now remember. And then he said that he was tired and that he had to go, he had to leave. I went over to him and sat in his lap and hugged him, and hugged him again, begging him to stay longer. He smiled a little sadly and said that he must go.

That is all I remembered the next day.

When I awoke, I knew this had not been an ordinary dream, a psychological dream. I knew that I had really been with my father, that I had met him in another place, a place not on Earth.

Years later, walking down the street one day, I felt his presence walking next to me, and we conversed. I heard him speaking, not outwardly, but

1

more telepathically. I believe he was telling me that he was going to yet a different realm.

Shortly after this I had another Dream. In the segment of this dream that I could remember, I was on a train. Trains for some reason often show up symbolically in these "other realm" dreams, either conveying the passage of time or that the loved one is changing realms, going to a different realm – or that we are changing realms or changing consciousness – and I knew that my father was outside the train and that he had reverted more to spirit than the bodily form I once knew. And that my visit with him was over, I was going back to Earth.

Daniel

I was in my late twenties, teaching piano and giving concerts, when Christopher and I created an artists' commune on State Street. I had met Christopher in the bagel store one day. He was a violinist, disheveled and thin, about my age, and he had just arrived in town. He was homeless and broke, so I brought him home with me. Christopher came with all his belongings: his violin, which he wore by a strap from his shoulder, and a knapsack, which was filled with violin scores and his clothes.

My little house on Buffalo Street was too small for us, so we began to look for a house that we could share with other artists. The State Street house seemed perfect, and the rent was only two hundred dollars a month. I signed the lease, being the only one with an income, such as it was – and we moved in.

The house was of an unusual architecture, as many of the old houses in Ithaca are. From the outside the house was not spectacular. Mainly it was in disrepair. More tall than wide, it had two gables with light-coloured stone mosaics and some scroll work, and a good sized wrap-around front porch. Stained glass windows formed the top panes of both front rooms; a small roof to the third story jutted out perhaps six feet and formed a balcony of sorts. Even from the outside, doors and windows seemed to be everywhere, in the most unlikely places, giving the house the overall helter-skelter appearance of a house you might find illustrated in a volume of fairy tales.

It was the interior of the house that most intrigued us. We first entered a glass enclosed entryway with built-in seats and places for shoes and boots. Inside, a labyrinth of high-ceilinged rooms and oak doors opened into other rooms and unpainted oak staircases wound through the house seemingly from all directions. Stained glass windows threw their coloured patterns from above the front door and the landings, and rooms with hardwood floors seemed to materialize everywhere, tucked into corners and along hallways. Two large living rooms faced the street; their French doors opened out onto a wide hallway, lined entirely in oak. This hallway led to another hallway, which led past several more rooms, and eventually ended at the downstairs kitchen.

Upstairs rooms opened onto other hallways and staircases, and more rooms of different sizes and shapes seemed to appear wherever we turned along the meandering hallway. A trap door that led to an unfinished attic stood at the top of the staircase leading up from the kitchen. The back downstairs porch led to slate paths banked by low stone walls, from which wild columbine and vines in tangled profusion grew in spring and summer. These paths wound around the house to the street, and a field of red poppies filled the small back yard. There was a small patch of grass for a front yard, and a thick row of hedges, five or six feet tall, shielded the house from the busy street.

Christopher moved in with his violin and his knapsack filled with scores; I at least had enough possessions to fill my small front room just off the eastern living room. The room was perhaps ten feet by twelve feet in size. It held a single bed, and a small wooden dresser that I had brought with me – and not much else. The walls were painted a light creamy yellow, with a few scattered crayon marks, and various smudges and dents from untold past encounters with either humans or moving objects. I began to write Zen koans and short poems on them in pencil. Eventually friends would enter and then follow the walls around the room, reading as they went. One door opened out onto the slate path which led to the street, another opened out onto the downstairs hallway. Christopher chose an upstairs room overlooking the back staircase. This was our new home.

Before long other artists asked if they could join on. Within a few months we had added a poet, a flutist, a writer, a calligrapher, a photographer, two additional violinists, a singer – and two painters who chose to live in the unfinished attic.

Soon both living rooms contained beautiful grand pianos, loaned to me by friends who had left town. The living room just off my room held my Chickering grand piano. A Steinway grand, a Mason and Hamlin grand and a harpsichord that friends had left with me for safekeeping were in the other living room. Both living rooms had window seats, which my students used while waiting for a turn at one of the pianos – later I was also loaned a Steinway upright piano which we put in the photographer's room at the end of the downstairs hall. During lessons I went from room to room teaching small groups of children. A visitor might enter the house and hear Czerny exercises coming from one room, a Mozart piece emanating from another and students playing duets on two pianos coming from a third room... with other students practicing their note reading in the window seats and quizzing each other with flash cards.

To try to organize the running of this large household, we made a list of all the chores that needed to be done weekly, and divided them up among us. The poet read his new and old poems in the kitchen while we prepared dinner, and the artists who lived in the attic sketched some angels by the telephone in the back hallway and painted us whenever we would hold still for them. The rest of us practiced our instruments, or followed our muse more quietly – with ample philosophic and artis-

4

tic discussions at all hours in the kitchen. Visitors were a constant source of companionship and interest. The rent per person when the house was full was less than twenty dollars for each person, and some of us still struggled to find enough money to pay it. Often some of us would pay someone else's rent as well as our own.

It was here that I met Daniel. Tall and thin, handsome – with dusty blond hair and deep amethyst, almost purple eyes – Daniel was a friend of one of the painters upstairs. We spoke occasionally, but had no true conversation until the night before he died. And that was only because I generally stayed up late, sometimes until dawn, reading or practicing or meditating, long after everyone else in the house was asleep.

Daniel came into my small downstairs room well after midnight that night. I looked up from whatever I was doing to see him in the doorway, half in and half out of the room, leaning on the doorframe. He wore a haunted look that pierced my very being. He smiled sadly and quietly asked if he could come in, if we could talk. Then he began to speak, first in sentences, later in fragments. At one point he began to cry. Later he both cried and raved, and paced my room, and paced the room again, walking a few steps in one direction and then abruptly turning back – as though physical movement would somehow allow him to escape the torment of his thoughts. This went on for hours. He talked about his life in broken sentences – his disappointments, his fears, his anguish – occasionally he would wait for me to speak, or would ask me poignant questions. But as the night wore on I existed less and less in his troubled world, as though I slowly faded as he became more and more trapped in his own thoughts. At one point he took the blanket off my bed and wrapped himself in it – and then he continued pacing the room, wrapped in the blanket, draped in it like an old wandering mendicant or monk unsuccessfully warding off the cold. He was mostly incoherent now – although fragments of rational thought still remained here and there – and finally he became angry, and easily put his fist through the plaster wall. That slash was there until I left the State Street house, a constant and painful reminder of that night. Near dawn, he began to repeat that he wanted to start life over again, he wanted a new body and he wanted to start over. At this point – it was now five in the morning – I woke the whole house, going from room to room, telling everyone to wake up and meet me in the kitchen because Daniel was going mad.

He was taken upstairs and put in someone's bed while the rest of us sat or stood around the kitchen table, half asleep and half dressed, and discussed what course of action we should take. No one around that table knew exactly what to do. We struggled to find answers to a problem we barely understood, as we weighed the various solutions that were presented and voiced around that old wooden table – like counterpoint in

5

a Bach fugue – each voice listened to and compared with other tired and sad voices already spoken. The theme "what should we do" inwardly repeated in all minds, minds barely awake, and our sad and tired individual minds wondered if all our minds could magically join, unite into one large mind, perhaps then the answer would emerge. We thought and spoke together until past daybreak, and it was finally decided that we would take Daniel to the hospital the following day in spite of any objections he might have, so that he could have the care he needed.

Then everyone went back to bed.

The next morning Daniel was gone. We hastily formed small search parties and began looking for him, setting off in different directions. Towards mid-afternoon we all converged at the house and in desperation set a specific hour to call the police if we could not find him. After this short house meeting, I suddenly became so tired that I decided to lie down and take a nap. Later I learned that everyone in the house had gone to their rooms, and had also fallen asleep.

As soon as I closed my eyes, a sort of "movie" made of richly coloured and changing images began to play in my forehead. I was not asleep, I was awake – and I knew that I was still on my bed in my small room at the State Street House. As the movie began, I stepped into it, until it became my entire world. I was now standing on Quarry Bridge, which was several blocks south of the State Street house. I was facing west overlooking the gorge, and Daniel was standing to my right. He was also facing west and he was looking over the railing, into the forest below. Christ was standing to my left.

Daniel was not aware of my presence on the bridge, but I tried to speak with him anyway; I told him that we were going to get him the help he needed – that all would be fine again one day if only he would be patient and give life a chance. I begged him to return to the State Street house, and even tried to take his arm and pull him back from the railing.

Christ then came over to me. He began to speak and as He spoke I saw Daniel's entire life, and the Plan God had had for him – and what Daniel had done with that plan.

We were looking out over the gorge now, into the sky – and visions kept unfolding there, my life and the Earth's life and destiny, the destiny of all creatures of Earth and perhaps even of other realms – they all seemed to unfold with great precision and clarity in that sky over the gorge, and Our Lord waved His Hand across that patch of sky to change the visions there. And in those visions were condensed an untold number of words and images that encompassed the Truth and Wisdom of all lives and perhaps all worlds. This part of the vision I cannot clearly remember – as though Christ had put me in a higher consciousness to explain these things to me, a consciousness that I can no longer access.

Before I knew it, I was traveling very quickly through a dark tunnel. At the end of the tunnel was brilliant white Light, and I jumped, threw myself into the Light. This was long before I read accounts by people who had known near death experiences – I had never heard of this tunnel which leads to white Light when people "die."

I remained there, in the Light, for some time before the scene again changed. Now I was in a blue world; everything in that world was a beautiful blue I cannot describe, we do not have words to describe that blue. I was beneath Quarry Bridge, in the gorge, but I did not yet know where I was. I only knew that I was in a forest made of beautiful blue Light. And Daniel was there. He was laughing and running towards me; he was as joyful and exuberant now as he had been agitated and tortured the night before. We hugged each other with relief and love and then began playing a children's sort of game, like tag, chasing each other and laughing in the forest, hiding behind trees and playing with childlike joy amongst the beautiful blue trees and ferns and wildflowers under the bridge.

And then the scene changed. The world was no longer blue. Now I was sad and alone in the gorge under the bridge – and I knew where I was. I now saw Daniel's body lying on the ground, where it had fallen from the bridge. And the sudden realization came that Daniel had jumped from Quarry Bridge. And that I – in some mysterious way – had jumped with him.

As I tried to understand all this, something again abruptly changed. The world was still its normal colour, except that now it seemed again to be made entirely of Light, this time white Light instead of blue – clear, radiant Light, Light of a crystalline clarity and intensity. I looked around me, filled with wonder and awe. Daniel's body was now a bit farther in the distance, still face down on the ground. And as I gazed at the body lying so still and inert on the bed of the gorge, another more transparent Daniel arose from the body lying on the ground and began walking away from me into the distance. Where he was walking was in a different realm, for he was walking towards a different horizon. This new horizon had no spatial relation to my world of Light in the forest at the foot of the gorge. And as he walked away from me into the distance, I was filled with an indescribable Love for him, greater than any love I had ever felt for any other human being or creature on Earth. An inexpressible Love for a young man named Daniel, whom I barely knew, and would never see again on Earth – a man walking into the distance without even looking back, for he was already in another realm and no longer aware of my presence. None of this mattered. I loved him in a way I had never before known, or even envisioned.

And as I stood there filled with this new indescribable and powerful Love – I wondered if I was in Heaven, where all beings love each other always, for the Love seemed to be everywhere. The trees were made of this Love, the stones of the gorge were this Love, the air itself was this Love. The Love was so strong, so powerful and all-pervasive, no negative emotion could exist, could even surface, in this place where I was now... and then I lost consciousness entirely, I must have fallen into a deep sleep.

When I awoke I was back on my bed. I went into the hallway and called out to the rest of the house. They came slowly and half asleep, singly and together, from their different rooms of the house into the downstairs hallway. I told them simply that our friend Daniel had done what we had most feared – he had jumped off Quarry Bridge.

One of the musicians called the police, to tell them that they should look for him in the gorge under the bridge. We were already crying when the police came to tell us that they had found him there. While the police were questioning us in the kitchen, someone took me aside and whispered that Daniel's fiancé planned to throw herself off Quarry Bridge, and that the painters and the poet had gone to bring her back.

I hardly knew this young woman. She did not live at the State Street house with us. Someone from the house had telephoned her, and she had joined the search parties and waited with us in the kitchen for news of him. She was a bit younger than Daniel, perhaps nineteen years old. The painters and the poet brought her back to the house and put her in my little front room with the Zen koans penciled on the cream-coloured walls and the gash left by Daniel's fist. She had fainted, and they so very gently and tenderly draped her onto my bed. I can still see this, as though I am still standing in that room. The poet leaned over, and gazed at her with indescribable Love. The rest of us stood in the doorway or in the hall or in the room itself, each in our own thoughts and feelings. I inwardly knelt before the scene – because it was a continuation of the tragedy and yet it was life here on Earth, life under our earthly sun and not in the shadows and gap left in our minds by Daniel.

We left the painters with the young girl, and went into the kitchen to outline our future plans. We quickly decided that the young girl was never to be left alone, and that we would take turns being with her – every hour of the day and night. We drew up almost equal shifts around the clock, and divided them up amongst us. I believe I chose two a.m.

to five a.m.. At five a.m. I woke another person in the house and at 7:30 a.m. she woke still another. We did this every day for at least a month, perhaps longer.

Looking back now, I see that this plan was partly a way of showing our love for Daniel and atoning for our mistakes with him. At the time, I don't think any of us consciously saw this – I certainly did not. We only saw the young girl who now wanted to end her own life, and we wished to prevent it. Most likely in today's world, we would have gotten the sweet young girl therapy. But that was not the first solution in those days; it was still a fairly untried avenue. We were ten or so artists, struggling with our art and trying to make a living from it, young and inexperienced in life – thrown together for the sake of security and companionship, now facing the aftermath of one tragedy and another potential tragedy, all in the same day. The day before, my most pressing worry and gravest responsibility was to not play the Liszt Hungarian Rhapsody I was working on too fast for my fingers to articulate clearly – and suddenly I had lost one human life in my temporary care and might now lose another. And this was true for every person in that house. The painters, the poet, the calligrapher, the photographer, the other musicians, the writers – we had all lived until this day, in a world under our control, in our art forms. The painters' world was in their canvases, the writers' in their notebooks and typewriters, the musicians' in their scores – we had all walked through a new door together, and were already on the other side of that door, trying to accustom our eyes to the new light and our feet to the new floor and our surroundings – which were vast and dimensional compared to the world we had now left behind. Yes, the decisions came easily now – the young girl would stay with us and be watched day and night for however long was needed. But beyond that easy decision were landscapes and paths and cities, inwardly and outwardly, that we had never seen, never been to. There was no conscious map we had followed to get there, we had fallen in and over the doorstep, each in our own way, with only our good intentions and our hearts both open and torn asunder by the day's unfolding occurrences.

I began to write songs for Daniel, a song cycle. The calligrapher looked up the symbol to summon the angel who prevents suicide in an old book he had, and drew the symbol on the door to my room. The painters in the attic painted new pictures of angels, this time on the walls of the kitchen, where the young girl spent many hours of each day.

I began a new Chopin Etude, his last etude, which was published posthumously. And still when I perform or play that piece, I am torn between realms with Daniel. Parts of it I still play almost like a lullaby – a lullaby between worlds, as though rocking all realms to sleep, into

9

Peace. This poignant sadness builds incredibly in intensity and volume in one section, but the triplet motive remains, and I stretch it in this section to bring the intensity of grief to its utmost, before it again drifts back to its beginning motives and melodies and quiet sadness.

Our worlds would never be the same. Perhaps we had left our youth behind. Perhaps we intersected briefly for this one unstated purpose and no more, as a path we traveled together for however many paces and miles before parting. For myself now, it feels more like a past life than a portion of this present lifetime, or events in another realm more than a portal within this life.

I cannot speak for the young girl or for the others that lived in the State Street house during those months. I had never doubted that we existed, in some form, as pure spirit, before we came to Earth. Nor had I ever doubted that we would travel to other realms after our lives here were finished. But if I did have any fear or doubts about the eternality of the soul on some deep, half-conscious level – they were forever quelled, extinguished, in this experience with Daniel.

My own transformation took many years to understand, if I even understand it now. I had been clairvoyant even as a child – but now the emotions and thoughts of others became a physical presence, a physical experience for me. I began to feel the energy currents in a person's body more clearly than I felt their physical frame. If I put my hand on someone's arm – I will feel their inner energy more strongly than I feel their arm. The term for this I discovered some twenty five years later. It is called clairsentience.

We think that our thoughts and unexpressed
emotions are private, and that they therefore
have no effect on the world around us,
but this is not so. They might be unspoken,
but they radiate out into the universe.
We are setting an energy force in motion with
our thoughts and the emotions that arise
from those thoughts. That force must
then obey certain natural laws of action
and reaction. The world, in this sense,
is what we humans make it.

At its highest, clairsentience helps me to distinguish between the thoughts and emotions a person carries and the life and communications of the soul. I might say that this clairsentience, combined with my clairvoyance, often allows me to consciously communicate soul to soul rather than through words or by the usual avenues of the personality – i.e., through speech, emotions, thoughts, behavior. We all communicate soul to soul; we are all deeply connected on the soul level. But in most people this connection and interaction are not conscious.

My clairvoyance eventually helped me to see through this material reality to the substratum of Divine Light behind it, the Divine essence of this universe.

How this quality of clairsentience arose from my experience with Daniel I do not know. I only know that it is connected in some way to the place I entered in the spiritual Heart, after I jumped into the radiant Light at the end of the tunnel, and after experiencing the blue and clear realms of Love and Light.

It was also after my experience with Daniel that I became a Divine Healer. At the time I was not aware of any new Healing ability. My first miracle came a few years later, with my little cat Nell. This I speak about at length in my first book[1], and is another discussion entirely.

> *With this understanding of Divine Healing,*
> *I was now able to send Healing to the*
> *darkness and pain I saw in many*
> *of my fellow humans, rather than recoil*
> *from it, or take it into my own being.*

---

1 *The Spiritual Life of Animals and Plants*

The Monk

All that winter at the State Street house, I read and carefully studied one Zen koan each night. I had found a small, thin volume of koans in one of the many bookstores in town. This slim edition contained valuable philosophic explanations and various "solutions" of each koan at the end of each short chapter.

I had not yet learned how to meditate. Therefore, it was extremely difficult and yet very exciting to try to understand these mind puzzles given to the Zen monks on their quest for Enlightenment.

At the end of each day I opened the small volume eagerly, and turned to the next enigmatic koan. And as the cold wind blew, or rain or snow fell outside the window of my small room, I sat alone while the world slept, first trying to solve the mystery before me on my own, and then turning to the various answers that Teachers had given their monks in the monastery, throughout the history of Zen.

Midway through that long winter I began to have repeating "dreams." Repeating in the sense that I always went to the same physical place in the dreams: a vast building at the top of numerous light coloured stairways that I would climb. These dreams were always in colour, and extremely vivid and clear. It felt as though I were truly there – and I experienced them with the clarity and logic of waking state consciousness. I could feel the steps under my feet with such surety and clarity that even now, almost thirty years later, I can still feel them under my feet.

The dreams always began at the base of the same long staircase. The stairs began in one direction, and then further up the staircase they angled in another direction. These angles never changed from dream to dream. I went up the many steps quickly and easily, and always with a deep feeling of anticipation.

Each night I met a man of Asian origin at the top of the long staircase. He always stood there waiting for me to arrive at the top of the steps, and he always wore the same maroon coloured robes.

Immediately upon reaching the top of the staircase I would wordlessly follow this man to the left, along a fairly narrow passageway outside the vast building now on my right. We never spoke, yet I knew that he was taking me to someone of great importance to me, a person somewhere in that huge, many-roomed building. The next morning this was all I could remember of the dream.

I revisited this dream so often that I also began to be aware of, and recognize, the surrounding countryside and other, smaller buildings nearby. I could not identify the town or even the country I was in, although I knew it was somewhere on this vast Earth and not in another realm. Some nights I passed other people on the stairs, at other times I seemed to be alone on the vast staircase. In time, I noticed that other staircases also led up to this huge edifice. One long set of steps led away from the staircase I was on, and others were still farther up the building, to my right as I approached. Some nights I ran up the steps, I knew them so well. And over time, the overriding feeling I had when I arrived there was one of pure joy and anticipation, familiarity. And this is all I ever remembered the next morning – seeing the man in maroon robes patiently waiting for me at the top of the staircase, and then climbing or running up the endless steps to join him.

By the following winter, I had joined the meditation center[2] in Valois and had learned to meditate. The meditation center was an hour or so from Ithaca, over some difficult country roads and we often braved snow, sleet, fog and snow to get there. After meditation we were served homemade soups and breads, and then began philosophy classes that often lasted until ten p.m. or later. Two philosophy students had just returned from a pilgrimage to the Dalai Lama of Tibet. One cold, snowy night, the slides they had brought back with them were shown. The lights of the narrow log cabin were dimmed, and the projector began to throw its images on the small screen at the far end of the room. Soon I was deeply touched, for in one of the first images, I saw the handsome man who had waited for me so patiently at the top of the stairs in my dreams. He was still wearing his maroon robes, and I realized with a jolt that he was a Tibetan monk. For in the photograph he was walking alongside the Dalai Lama who was wearing the same robes.

Interestingly enough, after viewing this slide show the dreams ceased and never returned. Perhaps because not long afterward I met the Dalai Lama in person, in waking state consciousness, on his first visit to the United States. He came to our meditation center in Valois more than once and we met with him many times, both in this country and in other countries around the world.

The rest of this mystery was solved when I perused a volume on Tibet one day and came across a photograph of the Dalai Lama's former residence in Lhasa – the Potala Palace. I stared at the familiar building and countryside with the shock of amazement – and joyfully gazed at the many white steps winding upwards, the steps I had myself so often climbed while in dream state.

---

2 *Wisdom's Goldenrod*

The Sister

I never met Marilyn's sister while she was embodied on Earth. Marilyn is a good friend and was my piano student. Both her parents died when she was young, and her older sister had taken care of her. She was the only family Marilyn had really known for the greater part of her life.

One day after her piano lesson, Marilyn mentioned that her sister was very ill and in a good deal of pain. She had been on dialysis for many years, and was very discouraged because the doctors had said that not much more could be done for her. She would always be in pain. Knowing what this sister meant to my friend, I said that I would send her Healing.

This was early on in my healing studies. I had already had a few accidental miracles, but had just begun my studies with John Payne at the Foundation of Light in Ithaca, New York. At that time, I really did not have much experience in the world of Healing. That night I sat down at my kitchen table, which was just under the big window that overlooked the garden and cluttered with papers and letters either received or waiting to be written, turned on the small stained glass lamp I had made on a trip to New York City – and tried to clear my mind of everything but the task ahead. I sat there for quite some time, concentrating as deeply as I could, and sent Healing to this faraway woman who had taken care of my friend for so many years. I did this every night for about two weeks.

In time, I again became immersed in concerts and students and whatever other distractions or fleeting emergencies arose, hoping that the Healing I sent had worked. One day Marilyn came in for her lesson and afterwards mentioned that she would be gone the following week. She was going to see her sister in Florida for the last time, because her sister had decided to go off dialysis.

I was horrified, and asked my friend why her sister had made this decision. Marilyn answered sadly: "My sister said that for several weeks she had been free of pain. But then the pain returned, and she couldn't bear it any longer. She said that she prefers to die."

This news was devastating, for I realized that in those weeks I had so diligently sent Healing – the Healing had, in fact, taken away the pain. But because I had not continued, this remarkable woman had decided to end her life. I said nothing, but was now confused about Divine Healing, confused about what had happened – and very, very depressed.

When I reflected on the situation that night, I saw what a responsibility Healers have to those who come to them. I also saw that the Healing methods I had been taught were much more powerful and potent than I had previously believed – and a commitment not to be taken lightly. Being a beginner, I had with the usual beginner's zeal jumped in over my head, too quickly, with faulty thinking and without enough knowledge.

This would never happen now.

In that heartbreaking situation many years ago, I learned many, many lessons. And I instinctively knew that even if I had sat there that very night, and every night in the future, and sent Healing and removed the pain – it would not matter. The decision had already been made, and Marilyn's sister would now abide by that decision.

Marilyn left for Florida as planned, and not long afterward her sister appeared to me in a corner of the garden. She looked somewhat like a transparent version of my friend – she was young, healthy and radiant, entirely made of Light... and very, very happy. She smiled and smiled at me, and I think that she had come to both thank me and to reassure me that in her case all had been for the best. She was now in a wonderful realm – the reward for her suffering and for taking care of her younger sister, as well as for all the other good works she had performed while on Earth.

She stayed a bit and then left the garden, and I never saw her again.

And this might sound strange, but in
that short and vivid meeting, which I
still remember very clearly and distinctly,
I felt a tremendous Love and a deep
connection rarely found on Earth,
even with my oldest friends.

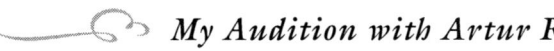

I began my musical studies in piano when I was a few months more than five years old. Within a few years I was playing difficult pieces: Mozart Sonatas, the Mendelssohn and Grieg Concertos, Chopin Preludes and Etudes. As I studied my various new pieces, my teacher would suggest that I listen to recordings made by the great pianists of our age. When I began my first studies of the Preludes of Rachmaninov, she suggested that I listen to the great pianist Artur Rubinstein.

Even as a child I was deeply struck by the beauty and depth of his playing. I was entranced and transported by both the music and Rubinstein's mastery as a pianist – especially the passion and the clarity of his playing. In addition to some shorter compositions scattered on various records, my parents had one vinyl Rubinstein recording entitled *The Heart of the Piano Concerto*. This recording had only one movement of several of the most beautiful piano concertos ever written. I had heard these concertos played by other, lesser known pianists; we had those recordings as well – but Rubinstein found patterns and hidden melodies in even the most brilliant and technically challenging sections of music. Every note made sense, every note was where it should be in relation to the other lines and other notes, both in time and space and in emphasis and phrasing.

I immediately took him as my teacher inwardly, and mentally noted his interpretation of various sections and phrases of the music. This deep admiration and respect for his playing continued throughout my training, and continues to this day. In fact, I could say that his mastery at the piano is one major reason I decided to become a concert pianist.

My audition with Artur Rubinstein occurred when I was in my late twenties or early thirties, and about six months after he had "died."

I met him in dream state. In the "dream," I found myself entering a darkened concert hall from the back of the empty auditorium. I can see and sense the hall now, as I write this: the worn plush seats with metal backs in their slightly curved lines reaching the aisles, the old comfortable and familiar feeling of an empty auditorium, the wooden planks of the stage... there was only one bright light, and that was onstage.

A beautiful grand piano was center stage, lit by the lone spotlight, and Rubinstein was seated to the left of the piano bench on a separate wooden chair.

I quickly walked down a side aisle, climbed onstage and sat down at the piano. I actually half-vaulted onto the stage from the orchestra pit, to

16

Rubinstein's surprise and amusement. The dream is still so vivid, all these years later, that I can remember every detail clearly – including the somewhat musty smell of the hall. Rubinstein said a few words to me that I now cannot remember or then could not hear, but I assume that he was asking me what I wished to play, and saying some words to put me at ease. I knew that I had come to play for him – this meeting had been prearranged, even to the time, for he looked at his watch before we began.

I put my hands on the keyboard and my hands began to play a piece that I had never studied here on Earth – a very difficult piece, a virtuoso encore sort of composition that the great pianists often play in concert to show their technical and musical ability.

At the time I did not know what piece I was playing – for the simple reason that I wasn't allowed to hear it. There was no sound as I played. I could only watch with amazement as my fingers moved with such incredible rapidity over the keyboard that they were almost a blur, playing a piece I had never studied – and I tried to stay relaxed and hoped that my hands would continue to know what to do until the end of the piece.

When I finished playing Rubinstein again said something I could not hear, and I slowly left the auditorium the way I had entered it. I was very, very disappointed, as though I had somehow failed – even though I still did not know why I was there, or why I had played for this great pianist.

It was perhaps a few weeks or a few months later, in once again reviewing the dream and analyzing the patterns my fingers had played on the keyboard, that I realized I had been playing the Spinning Song by Felix Mendelssohn. I searched through my scattered stacks of music and found the piece in an old uninvestigated volume with brittle, discoloured pages that I had probably found at a garage sale. I put the book up on the piano rack, and opened to the page and tried to play the piece.

I couldn't play it. I would have to study it like any new piece, slowly and carefully, analyzing and memorizing as I went. In other words, to learn it well enough for performance would take the same amount of work and time as any other piece I would study here on Earth.

Astonished, I then concluded that we all have tremendous, unfathomable abilities in our areas of study and work, and undoubtedly in other areas as well, that we are not even aware of. Perhaps we humans call this "potential" or the "collective unconscious," i.e., an unconscious portion of the psyche that contains all the world's knowledge. I would rather say that these abilities and knowledge are imprinted upon the soul, found within the soul itself, and therefore available to the psyche. And in waking state consciousness we can sometimes, often, perhaps, contact the soul in some way and draw genius from the Source itself.

I also began to wonder about the nature of dreams. I began to distinguish between my ordinary dreams, which were grey-coloured and often very confused – and special, vibrant dreams, that seemed so very real and were often later proven accurate in waking state reality.

Now when my friends said they had heard me give a beautiful concert in their dream, and described what I played and even what I wore with such amazing detail and clarity – I wondered if I had, in fact, truly given it – in another realm and in another consciousness. Had we actually met there, my friends and I, in that other realm, for that express purpose?

Another year or so went by before I again thought about the "dream" where I played for Artur Rubinstein in the empty auditorium. Still puzzled by my feelings of failure, I suddenly realized that it had been an audition – and I had not been accepted as his student. I clairvoyantly sensed that it was probable, or at least very possible, that many other pianists and teachers in towns and cities across this globe we call Earth had also been auditioned, and many had gone to study with the Master in another realm. I, on the other hand, was told to stay where I was and finish out my destiny here on Earth.

Alyssa was a talented piano student and a good friend. She began her piano studies later in life, perhaps in her late twenties. She had studied flute in the past, and with that training behind her she progressed rapidly at the keyboard. Within a year or two of study, Alyssa attained a remarkable proficiency at the piano. In spite of this rare attainment, she one day announced that she had decided to put all her energy and attention back into her study of flute. I respected her judgement and readily agreed to her decision. Students often came in and out of my studio, hopefully wiser and richer in their understanding and love of classical music.

Years went by, with little if any outer contact between us. Then the sad news came that our lovely Alyssa had "died" in a highway accident. She was still young, in her early thirties, and the news of her "death" was a terrible shock to all who had known and loved her.

One night a few months later, I had a dream, a vivid dream, about her. We were in another realm, and the "dream" was in beautiful, vibrant, transparent colours. The entire dream was infused with a radiant Light not found on earth, a Light that was both brilliant and crystalline. In the dream, Alyssa was showing me an intriguing array of pitched percussion instruments that do not exist here on Earth. Some were very large, with long chimes almost the height of the room, hung from the very high ceiling and nearly reaching the floor. These chimes vibrated with a most beautiful sound and resonance, and they produced sounds and effects I had never before heard or imagined. Other percussion instruments were placed horizontally or slightly tilted on frames, like keyboards – and Alyssa excitedly showed me the various instruments, and spoke about each one at length both before and after she played it. You might say I was being given a lesson on them. Some she played with cloth-covered mallets, others with metal ones, some only with her fingers. It was obvious that she already had a certain proficiency on these instruments of another realm.

She looked more beautiful and radiant than ever, there was a new glow and Light about her. She was composing music for these instruments, and perhaps also playing and composing music for other instruments not in that room. As she played and illustrated the various chimes, it almost seemed that the sounds these instruments made reached and vibrated into an infinity of realms and dimensions of sound and tone – something that cannot happen here on earth. It was also as though their sound was visual as well as aural – this I cannot find words for.

When I awoke the next morning, the "dream" remained vibrant and

19

real, and I inwardly knew that we had truly met in another realm. I also knew that I had gone to find her in her realm, and that it was a pre-arranged meeting. For she did not come to get me in the "dream." Alyssa did not lead me to that room – instead, she was in the chime room waiting for me. She was playing those beautiful instruments when I arrived, as though practicing or warming up for a concert. And when she saw me, after a quick smile of greeting, she began her guided tour of the room and her demonstration of the instruments without any hesitation. It was also clear that there was a time limit to our visit in that room, for she told me nothing else about the realm she was in, or her life there – our entire meeting revolved around the instruments. When I say there was a time limit, it might be that someone else had scheduled a time for that room after Alyssa. It is only in the lower realms that life is chaotic and disorderly.

In the higher realms, there is a solid and orderly frame for our existence, just as there is in this realm. Realities line up in those higher realms and, in that one sense at least, life there is similar to our life on Earth.

Intuition tells me that there was more to our visit. I suspect that Alyssa showed me the realm she was in and many other things as well, but all I consciously remember is what I have written. It could be that I was in a different consciousness for what followed, or that I was most interested in the instruments, so I remembered only the chimes. Then again, in the clairvoyant's world we find out early on that we can see only what we are allowed to see, and can only remember what we are meant to remember.

> *Then again, in the clairvoyant's world we find*
> *out early on that we can see only what we are*
> *allowed to see, and can only remember*
> *what we are meant to remember.*

I have written about my meetings with the Dalai Lama and his monks in dreams that one winter at the State Street house. These two meetings with sages are of a different sort. This time they are clairvoyant meetings in waking state consciousness.

One was with the Hindu Sage or saint, Muktananda. A friend and I were driving to New York City, and on the way we stopped at Muktananda's ashram in South Fallsburg, New York. I had never been there, and was almost overwhelmed by the throngs of people and the charged atmosphere of the crowded auditorium. When Muktananda first entered the hall, I was struck by his Light – it was of a sort I had never before seen, bright but with another added quality, a gentleness, a luminescence, one could say. He spoke and led chants that day. We spent some hours there; and then we continued on our journey.

The following week, or perhaps it was a few evenings later, I do not remember – I was standing in a friend's loft in Greenwich Village, looking towards the front windows of his apartment – when Muktananda appeared to me. He said nothing, just stood by the grand piano for some moments – and then was gone. Later, I found out that Muktananda had "died" the day of his appearance in the loft.

I was deeply grateful that I had been able to see him while he was still embodied on Earth, and amazed that he had come to visit me in the loft. I had only seen the Hindu saint from one of the last rows of a very large and crowded auditorium, and only during that lone visit to his ashram. I easily understood that he would have no trouble finding me. There is no "space" where he now is, and all beings are connected on the soul level. What amazed me was that Muktananda had come to see me at all. I did not, at that time, understand the power and omnipresence of a saint or sage, nor the strength and depth of their Love. Nor did I yet understand the nature of the vast commitment between Teacher and disciple, soul to soul.

The other meeting of this sort was with the Philosopher-Sage Paul Brunton. In the case of Paul Brunton, we met in a private interview instead of a crowded ashram, not too many years before he died – and about six months after I had joined the Center and learned to meditate. I had only read one of his books, a fascinating and illuminating volume about his experiences in the Himalayas.[3]

---

3 *A Hermit in the Himalayas, Larson Publications*

When I first entered the room for my interview, Brunton was comfortably seated in an armchair in an airy, sunlit room. He physically reminded me so closely of my piano teacher, George Driscoll – clairvoyantly perhaps for a moment they blended – that in those first moments of our meeting I almost stared at him in disbelief. The overriding feeling was that I knew this man, and I had known him for a very long time.

Frail and serene, glowing, quietly dignified, with
a very gentle, soft voice that was almost a
whisper, yet his speech carefully articulated –
this man changed my entire life during our forty-
five minute interview. He did not accomplish this
with words, but rather in some other mysterious
way that took years for me to understand.

I asked him one or two short questions, which he politely answered – and then we sat there in silence for the next thirty or forty minutes.

In this silence Brunton seemed to be reading my entire life and being. At one point he became quite ashen and gave me a few understanding words about my unspoken past. At the end of the interview he mentioned some events coming up in my future. In his presence, one did not need to speak.

At first I heard myself inwardly answering his unspoken questions, but then all thoughts ceased. I am embarrassed to admit that early on in this warm, full, inner and outer silence I put the thought: "I love you" in my mind, in a way, to test him – to determine if he read my mind, and to see what level our inner communication was on. In response, Brunton looked startled and then threw me a surprised glance. I smiled at him and inwardly said: "Sorry. I won't do that again," and then cleared my mind of all thought for the remainder of our interview.

Later in this meeting with Brunton, I was consciously standing in my spiritual Heart – the first time I remember this happening. My Heart and all that it contained was all around me in the room, surrounding me. I could do little more than look around at all that was manifesting from my Heart, intrigued and wondering. I did not understand, nor did I say anything. Brunton smiled at me, and very politely and very gently handed me a box of Kleenex that was on the small table next to him. My nose was running, although I hadn't noticed it, and I smiled and thanked him as I took a few sheets of tissues from the box. Then I continued to look about me, still wondering at what I was seeing and experiencing. And occasionally, when I remembered, I half-heartedly dabbed my face with the wad of tissues.

Near the end of the interview, Brunton softly interrupted our inner communication and initiated an outer, verbal conversation. He spoke of the piano and composition – which I had not mentioned – and at the very end offered: "What you are looking for is a step beyond music." And as he quietly said these simple words, I clairvoyantly saw what I was looking for unfold before me into what looked like layers of other, distant realms. The vision was indistinct however, as seed thoughts often are.

And then he pointed to me, shook his finger at me and said: "Meditate every day" – and he repeated this – "but not too much." He then said a few more words of instruction and concluded our interview.

My entire life changed after this interview.

Many changes in my life and being I could not even begin to articulate, but one very drastic change I might perhaps find words to describe. Prior to this meeting with Brunton, I had struggled with bouts of severe depression – caused at least in part by my clairvoyance and later worsened by the added clairsentience. Often, after a period of severe depression, I would read in our local paper that someone had jumped off one of the many bridges in town the day or night before, or some terrible world event had occurred. It took many years of training for me to understand and completely end this half-conscious empathetic, psychic, communication with my suffering fellow humans. I was taught how to help and heal others without this psychic level connection, by learning how to bring the clairvoyance to a higher level.

I had always felt this deep depression as a falling or plummeting into a vast inner space filled with despair. Shortly after my meeting with Brunton, I watched my negative thoughts and emotions forming in the usual way and braced myself for the fall into that vast, dark inner space. I did fall into it in the usual way – except this time it was not black, not filled with despair and emotional pain. Instead, I was met with beautiful and powerful Flames of Light and Peace and Joy emanating from the Spiritual Heart. Since that day, I have never once experienced that deep depression, the despair that had been so common in my inner life.

I then vowed that I would strive to perfect myself
through prayer, study and meditation, so that I
could one day help others in a similar way.

23

A few years later, some friends and I went to New Jersey, to hear the Dalai Lama speak at a Tibetan monastery there. It was a beautiful day, sunny and clear. The Dalai Lama spoke of many things: that we are not the physical body nor the small, personal mind; the Doctrines of Emptiness and Impermanence, and other wisdoms. As we were leaving, my Heart began to burn, my spiritual Heart filled with warmth and Light, and I could clairvoyantly see that it was glowing – there were images in the spiritual Heart that I could not make out, because the Glow was so strong. The people I was with were talking and laughing through my experience, and I was grateful that they did not attempt to verbally communicate with me just then, for I wanted to immerse myself in the glow of my Heart without distraction. After some time the Glow diminished, and I reentered our conversation, on the car ride back to Ithaca.

We later learned that Paul Brunton had "died"
that same day – and I could only conclude that
he was responsible for that Glow in my Heart. It
was, perhaps, his beautiful and temporary
"good-bye" to me, his parting Gift.

The Warning: Paula's Dream
and Inger's Prophecy

A few weeks before I "died," that is, a few weeks before my car accident – I was walking down the Commons with my friend Eleanor when a mutual friend came running up to us. It was our friend Paula, a fellow meditator and member of Wisdom's Goldenrod. On this particular sunny afternoon – it was a beautiful day – she met us with her usual smile, but there was an urgency and an intensity that I had never before experienced with her. "Laurie, I had a dream about you the other night," she said. "In my dream, you were walking down State Street.[4] An atomic bomb was above you, ready to fall on you. It was as though I was in your body, and knew you couldn't stop the bomb from falling or prevent the nuclear devastation."

For whatever reason, I did not take her dream seriously. In fact, I could not even take in what she was saying – perhaps because she had interrupted an interesting conversation with Eleanor and we were on our way to lunch, or because it was a beautiful sunny day in early autumn. Or because Paula is a sprite-like being and Eleanor was a being of Light, and somehow an atom bomb seemed very out of place with the scene as a whole. I lazily asked myself: "Why is she warning me with such urgency, if it cannot be averted?" Paula put her hand on my arm and said, "Laurie, you must listen to me. I know there is a reason I was given the dream." I began to see that my friend was truly upset, and perhaps I had better pay attention to what she was saying. Finally, in desperation, Paula again repeated: "Laurie, I looked up and saw that an atomic bomb was falling on you. I knew nothing could be done to avert a terrible and vast nuclear destruction. You must listen to me!"[5]

By this time Paula had given the warning so repeatedly and seemed so distraught that finally I just closed my eyes. Outwardly, I was standing on the Commons with my eyes closed, with quite a few strangers now looking on and undoubtedly wondering what was going on in our small section of the sidewalk.

When I closed my eyes and looked within I saw New York City after a nuclear explosion. The entire scene was transparent, composed mainly of clear Light, and so horrifying I could barely look at it. I somehow, by my intent, quickly turned time back in the vision and prevented the nuclear devastation. This took only a few seconds. When the inner vision ended, I opened my eyes and noticed that I was now complete-

---

4 *A block from where we were standing and only a few blocks from my accident, the intersection of State St. and Aurora St., Ithaca, NY.*

ly surrounded by an intense blue Light, a blue somewhat diluted by the Light, as though a bright sun were shining through a piece of clear blue stained glass – but still quite blue and extending from my body for quite a distance. In that blue cloud surrounding me, a bit away from my body, I could see indistinct events and happenings, emotions and many people. What I am describing here is not what some people call auras. This is more like a spontaneous inner burst, projecting the inner seed thoughts of future events outward into a limited band surrounding the person, and emanating from the spiritual Heart. These images are indistinct, as seed thoughts generally are. It is more like a capsule bursting, and the encapsulated events that are projected often begin to unfold almost immediately – and can cover a ten to twenty year period in that person's life. I had clairvoyantly seen this blue-coloured band of Light surrounding myself and others in the past, and it always seemed to bode deep suffering in the future for that person. I turned and smiled at my friend Paula and said: "Don't worry Paula, the nuclear attack won't happen. It's been averted, it won't happen." We said a few more words and parted. I thought no more about Paula's dream, almost as though it had been emptied from the continuum of my memory.

As an addendum, six or so months before meeting Paula on the Commons, a friend came by and said that she had been given a message for me, from my Swedish friend Inger. Inger had told her: "If Laurie is lucky, she will stand face to face with God within the year."

I had forgotten this as well.

---

5 *Twelve years later, when I was writing this portion of the book, I asked Paula about that day on the Commons. She wrote: "When I ran into you on the Commons that day, I was desperately late for an appointment and was trying to avoid seeing anyone I knew because I was so pressed for time. It wasn't until I stood beside you that the dream came back to me and I was surrounded by its full intensity and urgency."*

"In the dream, I was walking down State Street. I was aware of you walking down the street, but as if I was inside your body. I remember looking up at the sky and seeing a bomb descending. The physical appearance of the bomb wasn't significant, but I KNEW that it was a nuclear bomb. It was above you, ready to fall on you. I envisioned the devastation of cities that would ensue and can still see the razed buildings, devoid of any remaining human life. I still remember the dream so vividly. Most dreams fade rapidly from consciousness once I wake up, if I don't journal them immediately, they're gone. However, a few dreams have the flavor and staying power of wakeful consciousness. I remember them in the same way that I remember a significant event in my waking life. The dream about you had the same impact as an experience from my wakeful consciousness. I will never forget the dream. When I saw you, I was compelled to share it from a great sense of urgency. I'm not normally psychic, but I have had a small number of dreams and occasional experiences that were predictive."

As I will say in other sections of this volume, I personally do not believe in "accidents." If one accepts the belief that Divine Ideas run through every event, every occurrence, every meeting, every moment of every day – and that there is Providence in the fall of a sparrow – then there can be no "accidents," it is not possible.

My "accident" happened in a car. In this occurrence I "died," my heart and breathing stopped for some minutes. Afterwards, curious friends and acquaintances asked if I had had a mystical experience while I was dead. I could only answer that it was perhaps the only four or five minutes in my life when I had not consciously had a mystical experience. Whatever happened while I was "gone" was a complete blank, as though a heavy steel door had slammed shut behind me. Interestingly enough, I later found out that my close friend JF was speaking with a clairvoyant when she heard the news of my accident. The woman, who had never met me – in this reality at least – said: "She is gone, she's left. But she'll be back." And then she added that it was as though a Door had closed behind me; she couldn't see a thing.[6]

When I did (reluctantly) return to Earth, the shock was enormous. Returning to the body – is not always an easy thing. Leaving the body and Earth-as-we-know-it was very easy. The re-entry was not. When I regained waking state consciousness I was immediately and irrevocably surrounded by my own wrecked car, shattered glass and crushed, twisted metal everywhere, the twirling lights of police cars, many people I had never met, a physical body which I had recently and happily escaped from even if briefly, and chaotic NOISE. A babble of machines and vehicles and people and whatever else was going on at that time at that now very busy and upset intersection.

---

6 *I might also add here that this woman was a traveling gem and mineral merchant. JF was the co-owner of a metaphysical bookstore in town, and she had met with the saleswoman at her home instead of at the bookstore because there was not enough parking in town. JF was looking at the woman's wares at the time of the phone call, and her driveway was filled with crystals and other beautiful healing rocks and minerals. That I had already returned to Earth some minutes earlier is of no matter, for in the clairvoyant's world there is no time. The clairvoyant looks back into the past or sees the future with equal clarity – and we do not know what we are seeing in relation to Earth-time. We are going to that timeless place inside to retrieve this information, that place where the Divine Ideas are given to the soul. And in the framework of those Divine Ideas, my good friend JF was to receive the terrible news, for at that point no one knew the extent nor the seriousness of my injuries, while in the company of a clairvoyant and standing over a driveway full of beautiful healing crystals and other wondrous stones.*

One of my rewards for coming back to Earth was the man leaning over me when I first came back to waking consciousness. When I first opened my eyes, I was looking directly into his. All I knew and all that I owned in those first few seconds were his eyes – and they were very brown and filled with Love. Love and concern. Wherever I had been, I had not yet completely returned. I had no personal history in those first moments: no possessions, no memories even of my life on Earth, no home, no friends, no family. I only had his eyes. My first interaction with our planet, because of this kind and caring man, was his Love and Compassion for me. And in that moment I knew, I knew completely and to the depths of my being – that the only important thing here, in this reality, is Love, the Higher Love, the Divine Love that each creature should have for every other creature here on Earth. Nothing else matters, nothing else truly exists here. Nothing else here is truly Real or Eternal – only the Soul and its vast Love.

I closed my eyes and tried to pour that Love over the entire Earth.

When I opened my eyes again I could now see the scene around me, and hear the voices and other jarring and incomprehensible sounds surrounding me. I also realized that I could not move from the neck down, I was completely paralyzed. I closed my eyes again and when I could speak I asked the man with the beautiful brown eyes filled with Love to put the miraculous medal I was wearing around my neck in my hand. He had taken it from around my neck in order to get my heart and breathing started, and he apologetically rummaged around trying to find it. When he located it, he gently placed it in my left hand. I then inwardly said the prayer Our Lady gave us to say three times: O Mary, conceived without sin, pray for us who have recourse to Thee.

It pleased Our Lady to grant my request, for immediately I could again move. I was no longer paralyzed. It was a miracle. Months later, I offhandedly told one of my doctors that I was curious to know what might cause paralysis in an accident such as mine. He answered without hesitation: "You would have injured the next cervical down." I smiled at him and replied : "No, I did injure the next cervical down. I was paralyzed in the accident. Our Lady changed it."

There is one more thing I would like to add at this point in my narrative. Most of my friends avoided that intersection; some of them still do. Whereas I always enjoyed being back there, for the simple reason that I always saw many beautiful and bright angels still standing in that intersection, the intersection where I had the accident – *even a few years later.*

As they wheeled me into the ambulance, a little "movie" began in my head. Maybe because of my head injuries, I was unable to step into it until it became my whole world. Instead, it remained a more distant movie, as though I were sitting far back in the theater and not wearing my glasses. The movie was also twirling around in a wide circle, and fairly rapidly.

There was a single image in this clairvoyant "movie," and it looked like a Fax. And at the top of the Fax, written in very big, bold letters was:

REASONS YOU RETURNED TO EARTH.

The Fax seemed to be a few pages long, typewritten, and each page had numbered paragraphs. The first page had about five numbered paragraphs on it. Unfortunately, the Fax kept spinning and twirling around, because my mind was spinning around, and the Fax eventually spun off into the distance, before I could read anything on it other than the main heading.

From this I learned:
1. There were many reasons why I returned to Earth.
2. I was not supposed to consciously know what they were.

I have always had the feeling that while I was "dead," i.e. while I was in other realms, They told me everything – everything about my own life and Destiny – and also that of the world and its future, just as Christ had when I was on the bridge with Daniel. And for whatever reason, once again I was not supposed to remember what I had been shown. I can say, however, that as the events of my life and the world's life unfold, certain things do seem very familiar to me.

I am also very embarrassed to say that I think it was necessary to bribe me, that some negotiations took place before I agreed to return to Earth. I say this because too many lifelong dreams have come true since my accident: for example the beautiful seven-foot Steinway now in my living room, and another, slightly smaller Steinway grand in my studio. And other long-awaited gifts as well, too personal to discuss here.

It is also possible that I did meet God Face-to-face, as my friend Inger had predicted. As I have already written, I do not remember what transpired in those few Earth minutes. But the thought, the possibility always brings tears to my eyes – because the image of the Beauty and Goodness that is God always shows me my own poverty in the most jarring way, and brings the deepest Longing – the Longing to be worthy of it, to somehow stand in the Beauty of my own soul so that I may stand before this indescribable Purity and Light without flinching, without apologies. As it stands now, I feel unworthy to view that Goodness and Beauty, even for a fleeting moment.

I also think that I went to many places, on Earth and in other realms, and met with many different people during the time I was "dead." For example, perhaps I studied with Franz Liszt and Frederick Chopin for piano and composition. I possibly went to many realms, and met with many different people, for a variety of reasons. For even though I was "gone" for only five or so minutes of Earth time – in those realms, time is of an entirely different nature.

On September 11, 2001, I awoke to a telephone message on our answering machine from one of my meditation students. The message said that the World Trade Center Towers in New York City and the Pentagon had been bombed, would I say some prayers for the world. I said some prayers and then remembered that one of JF's relatives worked in one of the Trade Center Towers on certain days. I immediately phoned her, to see if he was safe and also to confirm if the news was true. JF had also received a phone call with the terrible news, and had turned on her television. She hastily put the phone down and returned to CNN's coverage – just in time to see the second tower hit by the second hijacked plane. I heard her say from across the room: "It's crumbling, the whole building is crumbling...." and she started to cry.

She came back to the phone and said that she wanted to try to reach her sister, so we hastily said goodbye. I ran upstairs and turned to CNN. For the next two weeks I watched CNN almost day and night, until the images and voices of the commentators became almost more important and closer to me than those of my family. But that first morning, as the horrible events unfolded, alone upstairs watching and waiting and listening – I was in a world of my own.

For as I watched the onscreen images of the Twin Towers falling, the frightened and injured people running down the street, the plumes of debris and smoke erupting like a nuclear cloud as the buildings fell, I was thrown back into the blue vision, with a jarring jolt, into another terrible, even more horrible scene. I was thrown back into the vision I had only glimpsed that day on the Commons, years earlier. Only now I was entirely in the vision. I was not seeing it from afar, from a distance – now it was my whole world. I was running down the same streets I was watching on the TV screen, only the streets were deserted. I was running down those same streets on the television screen all alone, with fires everywhere, in horror – there were no buildings, no people, only rubble and flames all around me. I could feel my feet on the asphalt as I ran, and I could feel the terrible emptiness of being so alone. I was reliving a flashback of a vision I had had years earlier, as though I were actually experiencing the events in the vision – and the flashbacks continued for weeks, always the same scene, running alone down those deserted streets with flames and rubble on either side and before and behind me. And the flashbacks happened even as I watched the images on the television; I was experiencing both at once – although the flashbacks seemed more real than what I was watching onscreen.

My personal reaction, after the initial shock of what I was seeing, was a sense of guilt and failure and great sorrow – that I had not been able to prevent the tragedy unfolding before me.

I was so shaken that I went into town and arranged to have lunch with some close friends. All morning I had heard or seen "Today, September 11th" repeated or shown over and over again on CNN's reporting – and at lunch I asked one of my friends: "When was my accident?" I knew it was in September, but I couldn't remember what day in September. One of my friends slowly said: "I was hoping that you wouldn't ask that. Your accident was on September 11, 1991. Ten years ago today."

Ten years before – to the day.

As the days went by, more than one commentator mentioned the possibility that the hijackers might have intended to cause a nuclear explosion but were unable to obtain the needed materials. Each time it brought back my meeting with Paula on the Commons and certain questions. Why had both my car accident and a nuclear attack on New York City arisen together in Paula's dream? Could my accident somehow be connected to a potential nuclear attack on New York City?

Still in shock, I asked myself if I had, in fact, helped to prevent a nuclear attack, as I had in my first vision on the Commons, perhaps paying the price with my accident and all the suffering that followed. The concept of suffering as ransom is not a new one. All of us will experience suffering in this life, at one time or another. If we choose to offer the suffering up for the good of others, for the world and its varied and countless inhabitants – it opens the Heart to Divine Love. If we instead choose to become angry or bitter or discouraged, this closes the Heart and brings more suffering, both to ourselves and others. Padre Pio refers to this sacrificial suffering as "a headache here, a headache there."[7] It is said that as Mary stood at the foot of the Cross, Her innocence and untold suffering freed countless beings in countless realms.

Undoubtedly I was not the only person running down those streets [8] through the conflagration, or inwardly trying to prevent it.[9]

I have more than once stood before Our Lady's statue in the church and said, "Use me." In other words, use me to help offset the sorrow and sin of the world. One manifestation of my clairvoyance is that I see sacred statues as though the Divine Being stands there instead of a stat-

---

7 *When someone once asked Padre Pio if his relative would be healed, Padre Pio replied that she would be healed, but that there would be "a headache here, a headache there" – meaning that others would unconsciously share in the healing by suffering pain.*

ue. And I have said those words when Our Lady has looked very sad, sometimes shedding tears that others cannot see.

When one examines the problem further, what would it take to turn back a nuclear attack? We would be asking angelic and Divine Beings to influence human minds and hearts – the human hearts and emotions and thoughts of the hijackers, perhaps their loved ones and associates, and those with access to the nuclear materials. If viewed in this light, it is not inconceivable that the selfless and altruistic intent and prayers of even a few good hearts and minds could prevent such a catastrophe. This, in any case, has always been my optimistic viewpoint.

Prayer is a thought and an intention, where we ask for God's help and Mercy. The great saints of all religions prayed continuously because they were always filled and surrounded with God – so their every thought and action was itself a prayer. Because of my clairvoyance, perhaps I am more consciously aware of the power of prayer. When I pray to a saint or to angels, I see them come. And often I am more conscious of where my prayers are needed, in terms of world events.

---

8 *Just as in shared dreams, one can share a vision of a future event and not be aware of another's presence.*

9 *A year or so after writing this manuscript, my friends Judith and Robert Ore spent a few days at Windgarth, our house on Cayuga Lake. For some reason we began to speak about the events of 9/11. Robert told me the dream he had the morning of the tragedy. His wife added that Robert had told her of the dream when he first awoke, before the event actually happened; he knew it was an important dream, perhaps a premonition. I asked Robert to write it down and send it to me. He wrote:"I was hovering over NYC looking at the GW bridge. A huge missile as large in scale as the George Washington Bridge was coming in to blow up and destroy. I had the desperate feeling of wanting and needing to stop it, but not knowing how. The next thing I knew there was utter devastation. Something major had collapsed. The city was in complete chaos: smoke, soot and devastation was everywhere. People were panicking, screaming and running frantically while I wandered through the murky streets. There were the skeletal remains of buses, cars, trains and giant steel frames sticking up out of the rubble protruding to heaven. This was the exact scene that I saw later that day as the scenes of the wreckage of the Twin Towers were broadcast! Never have I felt so helpless and hopeless. The next thing I knew I awoke still in the grip of this horror and related the dream to my wife Jude... About an hour later, as I was doing my morning routine, I turned on the TV to see the first plane hitting the Tower # 1! I screamed out to my wife "WHAT IS GOING ON?!" Sitting in disbelief as the scene unfolded! The reality of the dream didn't really hit home until the veil of smoke lifted from lower Manhattan...only to reveal the devastation that looked exactly like the images in my dream! I saw these events before they happened. To this day, every time they broadcast footage of that day and aftermath I am completely convinced that I was there as a witness to this devastation." –Robert Ore, Woodstock, NY*

But for the majority of humanity, who are not clairvoyant – whether you pray consciously or not, if you love your fellow humans or other creatures on this beautiful Earth, you will be where you are needed and when you are needed, on some level of your being, helping and healing others. This perhaps is highlighted in my friend Inger's interview, which comes later in this book.

After my accident, I lost my clairvoyance for many months. I had a good deal of amnesia – and actually didn't even remember that I had ever been clairvoyant. One of the most difficult aspects of those first few months of head injuries – was that everything looked so solid. I felt imprisoned by my physical surroundings. One afternoon my friend Eleanor happened to mention something about my clairvoyance, and I said to myself: "Oh, that's right – I used to be able to see through this reality." And I tried to see through this realm to another realm, for about ten seconds – and then I had to sleep for four or five hours. It was exhausting. Being born with clairvoyance, I had not realized that it was a mental power. Even now, so many years later, I have not regained some of the clairvoyant abilities I had before the accident.

After the accident, however, and for the first time – healing for others began automatically. The healing seemed to begin as soon as the request was given. Often there would be two messages on my answering machine, both from the same person: the first message asking for Healing and the second message thanking me for the miracle. I had never even heard the first message; I could still barely move. This, of course, was a tremendous Gift from God, because before the accident I had to concentrate as I sent Healing; it was not automatic at all. And this new Gift has remained with me, as have the other Gifts I have been blessed with during my brief history here on Earth.

The Falls

Three summers after my accident, Mariette came into the back garden and asked if I wanted to go to the Ithaca falls. Even though the falls are only a block or so away from our house, I had not been there since the accident. There are steep steps to climb, and I was still too injured. This particular day, however, after some prodding I said that I would go. I looked at my watch and said: "We'll go at 2:30." The reason I remember that I set the time and looked at my watch is simply that I never look at my watch, and even at the time I thought it very odd. So did Mariette. At 2:30 we left for the falls.

A fair number of people were there that day, sunning on the flat rocks below the cliffs, sitting under the falls, or swimming in the water. Mariette and I sat down on two large rocks some distance from the falls, but near the water's edge. It was a beautiful sunny day and I was grateful and happy to be there again after so many years. I inwardly began to pray.

Suddenly a colorful movie began to play in my head, and I stepped into it until it became my whole world.

I was now in a cathedral, and I was standing near a life-sized statue of Our Lady. Foreign soldiers, in uniform, noisily entered the church and grouped near the altar rail in a ragged line facing the statue. They were carrying machine guns and speaking in a language I could not understand. They spoke roughly, in short, abrasive sentences – and they did not seem to be aware of my presence. Their speech and gestures became more menacing, and I suddenly realized that they intended to shoot at the statue. Horrified, I ran towards the statue, to protect Our Lady with my body. As I did so, the soldiers fired their guns and a storm of bullets surrounded and penetrated me. In the inner vision, I fell to the ground and quickly died from my wounds.

As the inner vision began to dissolve, I quickly deemed the "death" I had experienced not only painful, but senseless – senseless because I had not been able to protect Our Lady. While still in that inner space, I decided to change the vision. I replayed the scene, but this time instead of running towards the statue, I asked Our Lady Herself to change the outcome. As I stood there in the church, the soldiers nearby at the altar rail, I asked Her to protect Herself and prevent the attack. In this version, the soldiers said a few more words to each other and then quietly left the church. The colorful movie in my mind ended, and I opened my eyes. Some young people were now in the water and making a good deal of noise. I looked over at them and saw that they were teasing a dog, dunking the dog in the water and then laughing at him. The poor dog was scared and miserable, and my heart could not sit and watch the scene any longer. I stood up and walked to the water's edge, prepared to say something to stop the teasing, but also hoping that my presence alone would be enough to end the scene.

Without warning, everyone on our section of the flat rocks below the cliffs was suddenly surrounded with flying rocks of all sizes, traveling at incredible speed and with frightening force. They looked and sounded like machine gun bullets, whizzing by us on all sides and into the water. There seemed to be hundreds of them, cascading off and down the high cliffs above us, gathering tremendous speed as they fell and then crashed onto the flat rocks below. Miraculously, not one rock hit me, nor anyone in the water. I immediately looked over to Mariette, to see if she was hurt. She had been hit by some smaller rocks, and I inwardly asked that she and everyone at the falls be given the healing they needed. I looked again. Next to Mariette, where I had been sitting before I went to the water's edge – had fallen a rock which was large and heavy enough to have easily killed me.

Although shaken by what had just happened, my next thought was that Mariette and I had somehow come to the falls to protect the other people there; perhaps so that no one else would sit down where I had chosen to sit. The fact that Mariette had asked that we go to the falls that afternoon, and that I had said "Yes, at 2:30" – all seemed to indicate that our presence at the falls at the time of the rock slide, was not accidental. In all the forty years that I have lived in Ithaca, I had never heard of such a thing occurring at the falls.

My singer, Louise McConnell, came to visit me a few weeks later. When I related this incident to her she said: "Good. You changed it." Then she smiled at me, and I began to understand. Yes, it was the first time I had changed a vision involving my own life. In the second version I had turned the solution over to the Higher, and asked Our Lady to avert the disaster – instead of sacrificing my life in an unsuccessful attempt to shield Our Lady from harm.

I mention this incident for a few reasons, but mainly to compare it to the vision I was given while on the Commons years earlier. In the vision on the Commons, I was unhurt; the nuclear destruction was all around me. Somehow in the vision, I mentally turned time back and prevented the nuclear disaster. The vision was not symbolic, it was what I was shown: i.e. the nuclear destruction of New York City. If it had been a symbolic representation of my accident, in the vision I would have been killed in the destruction. I would not have been watching New York City burning, in ruins, all around me. In the vision given to me at the falls, however, I was seeing a future event symbolically, almost as though I were in dream state. I was not shown the cliff above us and the rocks falling onto those below. In the clairvoyant vision at the falls, I was in a cathedral with a statue of Our Lady and enemy soldiers. The cathedral represented the falls, and the machine gun fire symbolized the falling rocks. After the vision ended, I stood up and walked to the water's edge in order to help a poor innocent dog – not because I consciously knew that I might be killed by a rockslide. And by asking Our Lady to change the outcome of the vision, I was actually asking Her to protect everyone at the falls that day. In the vision, Our Lady represented all humanity. In this instance, I was also allowed to avert a potential disaster, for myself and others.

On the Commons, there were two future events to consider: my car accident and all the injuries I sustained – and a potential nuclear attack on New York. Both these events arose in Paula's dream. Both did not arise in my vision, however. My vision only concerned the possible nuclear attack. I changed the outcome of the vision, the potential nuclear attack, because I was conscious that it could occur. When Paula kept repeating, "You can't stop it," i.e. the bomb falling on me – she was correct. My own accident was never shown to me in that vision. Therefore, the possibility of averting it did not even arise.

One would have to ask why. Why was I not shown a vision of my accident before I got into my car that September afternoon, so that I could have avoided that intersection and my accident? If clairvoyance were a personal ability, a product of the personality itself, certainly I would have had a vision of it in advance. From the personal standpoint, very few of us would wish to be in a horrible car wreck. But clairvoyance is not to be summoned up at will. It is given to us, when and if needed. And if God wills or allows an event to happen, either for the good of that soul or the souls of others – He takes the clairvoyance away. Paula told me her dream very clearly and more than once on the Commons that autumn day. I was only shown New York City after a nuclear attack and only heard Paula say that there would be a nuclear attack – and afterwards forgot the entire meeting. Even now, as I write this, I do not remember her saying that a bomb was going to fall on me as well. Those words were erased before the words even reached my mind.

I was not supposed to know about my accident, consciously, in advance. I was given just enough information, just close enough to the surface of my mind, that the shock of the accident would not kill me permanently. And so that I could inwardly prepare for it.

My Singer, Louise

A friend stayed overnight at my house on Buffalo Street – and in the morning she said: "Who's the blond woman I dreamt about last night? She looked terrible." I answered: "She did look awful. That was Louise."

I met Louise in "dreams." By this I mean that for six months or more before I met her in this conventional reality, I had many dreams of her. In those "dreams" I was with her at her house, a duplex which she shared with her sister Jude. The first time I actually visited her at her home on South Cayuga Street, in this waking state reality – I already knew where everything was.

That could sum up my life with Louise.

When I think about her now, all these years later – for some reason I first see her high heeled suede boots at the bottom of the stairs, near the wall. Perhaps this reminds me that she was shorter than I, and when we walked down the street I had to slow my pace so that she could keep up with me. Louise was generally unhurried in her movements and speech – she was one of those people who thought before she spoke, and she had a certain shyness about her. Sometimes she seemed almost statuesque, as though molded into a beautiful pose or stance. She said far less than most people, but in those few words of honest self-reflection or analysis of a situation – some Truth or wisdom always seemed to emerge, in a way I could never duplicate, even with her before me as an example. She had one of the sunniest personalities imaginable – and yet one always felt a deep tragedy there as well, a sadness that added depth to her nature. Yet – it is her laughter that I remember most, her musical laughter.

Louise and I met in our late twenties, through her sister Judith, who danced with the Ithaca Ballet. Jude also taught in their ballet school, where I was a beginning dance student. Jude had the typical dancer's body and posture, and a most amazing quality and radiance when she danced. She was also an excellent teacher.

When I left the State Street house, I had nowhere to go. I must have mentioned it to Jude, because she invited me to stay with her until I found a new place, and it was there that I met Louise. At that time, I was looking all over town to find someone who could sing my songs. One day in Jude's kitchen – Louise smiled at me, and in her unhurried way quietly said: "I'm a singer."

Louise was also an artist and painter. She often spent hours a day painting various scenes, faces, and entire paintings on t-shirts, which she then sold. Some were surreal butterflies or faces, others were pointillist designs reminiscent of my 12-tone music, with no apparent subject; others were more French Impressionist in style, with hints of Manet or Monet. She would show me her newest t-shirt painting, laugh her wonderful laugh, and then point to a small line in the corner of the painting and say: "I love that little line." Or, "Look at this one" – and it would be an almost infinitesimal little maroon dot hidden somewhere in her newest painting.

When I first met Louise, she was singing jazz with her father's band and also rock music with some of the best musicians in town. Louise's voice was absolutely beautiful, and she was one of the few singers I have ever met who could sing my songs. This was even more impressive because Louise had never learned to read music – or perhaps not reading off the scores worked to her advantage.

At her suggestion, before a concert or a recording session we first made a practice tape of the songs I had just written. I read through them with her, playing her line on the piano as she sang, or occasionally singing with her quietly, an octave below. She then took the practice tape home and listened or sang along with the tape until she knew the pitches and rhythms by heart. She practiced my songs everywhere – in the car, at home, walking down the street, by the falls – I heard them everywhere. She brought my music to life, made it a living entity, and for this I am forever grateful. We rehearsed sometimes late into the night, and her little girl, Carolyn, would fall asleep under the piano. Carolyn went with us when we gave concerts as well, and occasionally we would be driving somewhere together and I would hear snatches of my songs coming from the back seat – from Carolyn, who also had an amazing voice. This was impressive since most of my songs are not only atonal, but written in the 12-tone system.

Louise sang all the songs I wrote, and we gave concerts in and out of town, made a few recordings which were then sent out to radio stations all over the world – and in that last year we also made plans for more recordings and concerts and some television shows. Our professional relationship was something one dreams about, where the qualities and personalities of two people complement each other in certain ways to add power and strength, and in other ways each builds on what the other offers – both the polarities and the unisons working to create a larger unity, a whole that could not otherwise exist. That she loved my music and that I loved her voice was the larger frame – but within that, the music and our lives and personalities brought vibrant and muted colours and contours, some daubed on with a palette knife, some painted with a brush, some traveling together and others apart, a changing tableau of swirls and colours and patterns, heavy and thin, swatches and paths in paint or watercolour or gouache – both personal and professional.

We went to New York City to visit friends and gave impromptu concerts in the Village, on street corners, at the Cloisters, on the Metropolitan Museum steps – I played clarinet while Louise sang in her light summer dresses, looking like a figure in an impressionist painting, her blond hair shining in the sun, her memorable smile. On one trip to New York, we gave a concert in a loft in the Village. I brought a few musicians down with me from Ithaca, and my friend Frieda improvised a dance to the music. Frieda was an unforgettable dancer that Isadora Duncan would have adored; she used the walls of the loft in her choreography and also a Stars Wars light saber that someone had left leaning up against the wall. A reviewer from the New York Times was there, and I never did see the review, but I can't imagine that even New York had seen anything like our friend Frieda the dancer.

I can still see Louise upstairs in her little front room with painted wood floors and a small stove, sitting comfortably before her t-shirts stretched over an easel, often wearing a brown and tan plaid shirt rolled up at the sleeves. While Louise painted, I would put Carolyn to bed and tell her stories of how one day we would go to Europe and be gypsies, or live on a houseboat – or I would take her to school in the morning in my little yellow VW, or to the Waldorf school meetings at night. Now, looking back, I don't understand why Louise wanted Carolyn to come with me; the only people at those Waldorf meetings were parents and teachers – and neither Carolyn nor I fit into either of those categories. But somehow I never questioned anything that happened. At the time, everything seemed to make sense, because the energy flowed so easily from one event to the next that I almost never paid attention to what the event, in fact, was. And we were somehow a unit knit together by my music and her voice, her art and our combined love for Carolyn.

A year or so before she left for other realms, Louise appeared to me in her soul state, beautiful and radiant and mainly made of Light. She looked like an almost transparent version of herself, in the prime of life – and filled with inexpressible joy. Smiling the entire time, she told me that she was leaving Earth soon, and she wordlessly asked me to take care of Carolyn. The appearance did not last long, perhaps for a minute or so. A few months later she phoned to tell me that her cancer had come back, and that the doctors had told her that there was nothing they could do to save her life.

Louise was in a hospital in Boston, where she and her husband were then living. Neither one of us was now able to travel, I was still much too injured – so we spoke on the phone. Louise's appearance in my kitchen was not conscious on her part. Consciously, she had many personal reasons to stay on Earth, primarily her family – which now included her little granddaughter, Elisabeth. I told her not to give up hope, and for the next however many months we talked about and made plans for the future, even in our very last phone conversation. The radiant being that Louise *is* had no qualms about changing realms. On the phone together, I was relating and speaking to both the radiant being that appeared in my kitchen, and my friend Louise who wanted to continue her life here on Earth. Being clairvoyant, you could say that I was having two conscious conversations simultaneously.

Friends have asked me why I did not tell Louise the truth of what I knew. My answer is that Louise knew the truth; we all know the truth on a deep level of our being. Conscious knowledge is not the only truth. I basked in the vision of Louise that I had seen in my kitchen, and drew from all its Light and Love and Peace even as I spoke to her in her final days. She took strength from it as well, because I somehow reflected it back to her.

Nonetheless, after our conversations, I would put the phone down and cry. I cried because in those last days and hours we could not consciously in words, say: "Goodbye, I love you, we will meet again in another realm." Not only was I losing the woman with the beautiful voice who sang my songs, I was losing a very dear and close friend who I knew could never be replaced by another.

After Louise left for other realms, Carolyn and I seemed especially devastated. We had trouble deciding whether the rest of the family were in denial, pretending they were fine – or if they knew something we did not. Louise's sister Jude finally said: "Call our brother Jim. He's really suffering." So I called Jim in California, and we spoke at length – but that did not really help either. In the end, I just wanted her to walk in the room and start rehearsing, or go with me into the gardens, share a meal, or any of the other myriad mundane things people do together during a day.

Carolyn came to visit me whenever she could, every other week or so. We sat on the downstairs couch for hours at a stretch, talking and talking about her mother, everything we could remember. Then we turned to our times together during Carolyn's childhood, and talked endlessly about our dreams of gypsies and houseboats and every other scrap of time or place we had spent together during her childhood. Then we turned to philosophy, and we discussed the soul and eternity, and the connections between souls and realms and eternity. Then we tried repeating every word we had said to her mother in the past year, and every word Louise had said to us – endlessly talking – trying to somehow mend the grief of her leaving and the immense, bottomless rift that was left by that wrenching departure. Neither one of us even ONCE, not even for a fleeting moment, saw Louise or felt her presence in those first horrible, long, endless, empty months. Not I, the clairvoyant who saw into other realms almost every second of every day and had endless encounters with beings *I had never even met* when they were in the body, never even knew their names ...nor Carolyn, who had an imaginary friend called Louis her entire childhood, and had called me on the phone recently to say that she had heard a cockroach scream, and felt she couldn't kill him. And then Mariette would come down the stairs and smile happily and say: "Oh, Louise is here, I can feel her Love filling the whole house." And Carolyn and I would just look at each other in despair.

And from this terrible experience with inconsolable grief I learned something very important. Mariette had only met Louise two or three times in her entire life. Yet after Louise's departure for other realms, Mariette was the one aware of her presence.

I sat down and thought about this difference of perception. I thought about it over a series of many days, and finally came to the conclusion that in our deep sorrow, Carolyn and I were somehow blocking our own awareness of the Love all around us. Our inconsolable grief was actually preventing us from contacting Louise, from feeling her presence and her Love.

On Carolyn's next visit, we began discussing this new subject. And over time, we both slowly began to be aware of Louise's presence.

Clairvoyance in one form or another seems to run through the entire McConnell family. Louise's daughter, Carolyn, had an imaginary friend named Louis in her childhood, which I always found interesting because my father's name was Louis. Louise's granddaughter, Elisabeth, also seems to have the gift of clairvoyance. After Louise left for other realms, Elisabeth, who was then three years old, came out of Louise's room looking rather sad and then asked: "Where are all the angels and fairies?" From what I've pieced together from snippets of family stories, almost all the McConnell women have some degree of clairvoyance. Louise had her share, as does her sister Jude.

One afternoon when Carolyn and Elisabeth were visiting, Elisabeth suddenly asked if she and I could talk. She was perhaps ten years old. This was a rare occurrence. Generally, we just talked, we didn't arrange a conversation.

Elisabeth was waiting for me on the living room couch, and I came in from the kitchen and sat down beside her. She seemed very serious, and I could see her trying to collect her thoughts, so that she could clearly frame what was on her mind. She finally took a deep breath and said: "Every night when I would go to sleep, since I was around three years old, grandma Weeze (Louise) would lie down next to me and stay with me until I fell asleep." She looked up at me: "I could feel her lying next to me. She felt solid, like this couch" and she began patting the back of the couch we were sitting on, with her hand to illustrate her point. I nodded – because Louise has a very physical presence when she is visiting from her realm.

Elisabeth then went on to say: "And then she stopped coming." And she looked at me with such a mournful and serious expression, that I thought she was going to cry. "When did she stop coming?" I asked, and Elisabeth answered that it had been some months now. I didn't know what to say, but I offered the possibility that her grandma had another, conflicting new assignment. And that perhaps she came to visit Elisabeth at other times during the day, or perhaps when she was already asleep.

Sometime last winter, Carolyn called me on the phone to tell me that she was pregnant, and that it was a little boy. She was very excited and happy, as was her husband. I congratulated them both, and then asked her what he was to be named. She said that they had decided on the name Ian.

Little Ian is now about a month old. Some months before he was "born," before he came to Earth to live, Louise began to bring him to me. Sometimes I would be reading, or writing letters on the living room couch – and I would look up to see them by the piano, little Ian playing with toys on the floor while Louise stood over him. The scene was very, very transparent – and full of Light. He had light hair and looked about two years old, maybe a little younger.

Sometimes she would bring him to me and let me hold him. And at these times, I could feel him in my arms as physically as the couch in Elisabeth's illustration. One sunny afternoon, I was deadheading roses on the old, immense climbing rose bush out front, by the rose arbor – I was clipping off the spent blossoms over my head with hand clippers – and as the blossoms fell to the ground, they often first gently grazed my face. I was a bit annoyed, but began to hear little giggles and realized it must be Ian. He apparently thought it grand fun – and after a time I began to laugh as well, for I knew Louise was there and had brought him for another visit. This time I couldn't see him, but he seemed younger on this visit, maybe ten months old. In fact, now that I think about it, in each meeting he seemed to be a little younger than he was in the previous visit.

Sometimes when walking down the street, I feel Louise take my arm, as she so often did while she was on Earth. I often inwardly hear her singing my songs, as though she were still in an inner room somewhere in my consciousness. Sometimes I hear her laughing, a transparent and joyful laughter; other times she walks before me as a bright, Loving presence – and occasionally gives me a hug, a hug that feels just as real as though she were still on earth and embodied.

In this new relationship there are no disagreements, no misunderstandings, there is only Love.

And as the years go by, I realize that I have come to deeply honor and appreciate this new relationship that we have: a relationship between realms, between one embodied on Earth, growing older and greyer – and one eternally young and in the subtle Light body of another realm.

And because Louise is in the soul in its pure state, our connection brings me to the joy and peace and Love that is my own soul and my true Being.

Betty Joan

Betty Joan was another radiant being with much Light. She had enormous physical beauty as well, and sang like an archangel – she had a wonderfully rich and powerful voice. And I most remember her beautiful smile.

Betty Joan was the mother of three of my piano students. When the children were very young, she used to bring me a bottle of aspirin along with the money for their lessons. Some days she brought me homemade soup or a sandwich, but most often she looked around my house to see what I was lacking, and then at some future time filled the gap. One week she and the children carried in a huge, metal filing cabinet that they no longer needed, for my music scores; another time a big, solid wooden chair for the kitchen. Another wooden chair came later on and there were generous presents at holidays and on other occasions.

When the children were young, Betty Joan was like a mother hen or a mother duck with her brood. Often she tried to keep her three daughters in a tidy unit of sorts, I suppose so that she could extend her love and discipline over them more easily. This I clairvoyantly felt and saw as a beneficent presence hovering over the entire scene. Sometimes she would prod them into joint action. One day in the garden, I can still hear her saying, in her musical voice: "Girls, shake the pansies out for Laurie, so that she'll have pansies next year ..." Often we went to lunch after lessons, and Betty and I spoke of God and the soul while the children watched wide-eyed and listened attentively as they ate their meals. Occasionally we would disagree on some doctrinal point – and she would smile her beautiful smile and then laugh, a singer's laughter that brings music with it always. Inwardly I began to think of her as a sister, a sister filled with radiance and goodwill.

When the children were older, they had several hours of lessons on Saturday mornings. On some holidays I was invited to their house several towns away, a big house filled with children and festive food and the bustle and activity that accompanies holidays when there are many people and much love. Over the years I slowly – in a way – became a part of the family.

When the two older children went off to college, they often came and stayed with me in my little house on Buffalo Street. I sometimes met them in New York City – and although the deep and profound musical ties continued, as time passed our student/teacher relationships began to transform into adult friendships. We have, throughout these many years, woven ourselves through each other's lives in many varied ways and places, each event deepening the connection and love between us. The youngest now lives in Ithaca, and we have lunch together almost every week, catching up on each other's news and talking about many subjects, both personal and philosophical.

In any case, one day I walked into my kitchen and Betty Joan was standing there, shining and transparent, and almost entirely composed of Light. As had Louise, she looked young and radiant, glowing with the health and the Light and Beauty that is the soul. She looked very, very happy and was smiling broadly at me. And as with Louise, she had come to tell me that she would be leaving for other realms within the year. She asked me to watch over her family, the children she loved so dearly. Again, there were no outer words; she never moved or changed her expression. As with Louise, there was no conscious dialogue, inner or outer. The communication was wordless, more telepathic, more a feeling and a sharing of Light. When one stands together in that Light, no words are spoken, yet everything that is being said is understood. She stayed there for some time and then vanished.

These visitations, these appearances from friends in the soul state, are initiations of a sort. The radiant, eternal Light and Love permeates me, and the visions can be recalled at any time; they are indelibly burned into my memory. I consider them mystical experiences, given to me in trust for the loved ones remaining on earth, and for my own deepening spiritual life.

I was not surprised then when the news came, some months later, that Betty Joan had inoperable cancer. In our last phone conversation, she said, "I am not afraid to die. But I am worried about my husband and the girls." We spoke about God and the soul together for the last time. At the end of our conversation she asked if I would speak to her husband and try to cheer him, for he was suffering deeply.

I mentioned her appearance in my kitchen to her, and Betty Joan did not seem terribly surprised. I have since spoken of our supernatural meeting to at least one of her children. And I hope that it has and will bring them some comfort, to know that their mother loved them enough to appear to their piano teacher and friend – to ask that I look after them always.

I might also add here that clairvoyance means seeing clearly – i.e. seeing consciously into other realms. The communication soul to soul between those who love each other, or even between perfect strangers, is continuous. That most people are not consciously aware of this deep interaction does not mean that it does not exist. For myself, the true relationship with others is on this deeper, soul level. And it is a relationship based on and made of radiant, healing Divine Love and Light.

 *Arushka*

I met Arushka one clear, sunny fall day on a small footbridge in Ithaca. She was holding a handkerchief in one hand and a small child in the other, and she was crying silently and uncontrollably at the far end of the bridge. After a moment's hesitation, I went over to her, gave her a hug – and asked her what the matter was.

She looked up at me and quietly said that she had just received news from Russia that her father had died.

Intrigued by her presence on the bridge and the scene before me, I introduced myself. She said a few words about herself and her life, and then asked me where I lived and what my profession was. I told her that I was a concert pianist and a composer and began to ask her various questions about her life in Russia. As we said goodbye, she invited me to visit her at her home. This chance meeting was the beginning of a close friendship.

Arushka loved classical music and had an impressive and rare collection of new and old recordings, and hardbound books that she had brought with her from Russia filled overflowing shelves in several rooms. Heavy draperies in bright and somber colors hung on walls and over windows, and curtains rather than doors separated many rooms. In one corner of the living room stood a large puppet theater, with a deep red velvet curtain and handmade puppets on wooden sticks. Her apartment was furnished with heavy yet simple wood furniture, and colorful throw rugs made a patchwork floor wending from one room to the next. One felt that it was always winter in those darkened rooms. With their high ceilings and original oak wood trim, one could imagine oneself instantly transported to Russia upon entering the front door.

The kitchen was lined with old wood cabinets with glass fronts, nearly ceiling to floor on some walls, with barely enough space left over for the plain heavy wooden table which stood in the center of the room. It was at this table that we often spoke for hours, sometimes long into the night in the dim light of a single lamp, speaking quietly and fervently on a wide range of topics, some philosophical, some more personal.

It was in this way that I learned of her extraordinary intelligence and of her rich and often tragic personal history – a life one might expect to find in a book, rather than across town or down the street in a small American town such as Ithaca.

She unveiled her stories in her softly modulated, musical voice. Her face I always found to be of a rare and transparent beauty, of the sort you might expect to find sculpted, or painted by a Dutch Master and hung on a museum wall. Her speech was heavily accented and phrased itself in the Russian order and emphasis, with the majority of the small connecting English words either placed incorrectly in the sentence or left out altogether. In spite of these difficulties, my friend Arushka proceeded bravely into important and lengthy sentences, and the import of her words was not lost with the faulty sentence structure – in fact, she almost seemed to use her lack of language to advantage, relying on the strength of certain important words to convey meaning that otherwise might be diluted by more words used in a more conventional manner.

And in this musical and unusual, poetic way of speaking over time I learned of her childhood. One evening she quietly told me that her parents had placed her on a train with many hundreds of other children when she was only eight months old. It was the onset of World War II., and she and the other children had been taken to orphanages in the north and east. She had remained in one orphanage until she was eight or nine years old. She spoke of the cold – the children had few clothes that fit or kept them warm – there was little food, and even less supervision.

She spoke of a little boy her own age. They had loved each other and protected each other always, even if in little ways – that they often shared their meals, which were sometimes only a small piece of bread between them – that they brought each other the comfort and love that was missing all around them.

One day a stranger who said that she was her mother came for her. Arushka pleaded with this woman, her mother, to also take the boy whom she had loved as a brother for so many years. But the woman would not listen, and Arushka's last memory of the orphanage was the boy running after their horse-drawn cart, crying and begging that the mother take him too.

These stories seemed to follow and lead into other stories endlessly, all told simply in her soft and musical voice. Then the topic would change to a philosophic understanding of these personal events, the deeper meanings, and how they related to what she was ultimately to learn in life. I was always amazed at her lack of bitterness and the depth of her understanding.

I later learned that many came to her for her advice and compassion.

After some years, Arushka moved to the country, amidst fields and paths – and a line of immense fir trees that guarded the narrow road to her house. My visits grew less and less frequent, for she now lived quite some distance from town.

48

It was not too long after my accident that I heard that Arushka was dying of cancer. I was still too injured to travel, so we spoke over the phone. After she left for other realms, I often felt the strong presence of Love and knew that she was near – and one night, perhaps a few months later I visited her in dream state, in another realm.

She was teaching there, and very busy helping those who wished to learn more before transitioning to yet another realm. She barely had time to look up or greet me, and could only give a brief description of her new life. I understood that this was not her final destination, but rather only a temporary assignment.

I also saw many beings, perhaps hundreds,
crossing over a bridge from other realms in
a steady, wide stream to speak or study
with her, or to be guided to other locations
and other "helpers."

Two Apologies – Stephen and Leslie

Our neighbor Stephen was an athletic, vibrant man in his early thirties when he suddenly "died" from a swift and fatal illness.

His house was on the other side of our back fence, so we saw quite a lot of him while he lived there. He and his wife were very sports-oriented, and they probably played every team sport I had ever heard of. He was healthy and muscular, and enjoyed being strong and physically fit. To balance this, he was sensitive and thoughtful, baked pies and cookies, cared for his houseplants like a mother hen, and was – in a very appealing and charming way – quietly fun-loving and somewhat shy. Of medium height and build, he had a boyish look about him, with his fine, light hair and wonderful smile – his sweetness was both endearing and unusual, especially in a man of his age.

We spoke over the fence, or visited each other for an evening, or did various house projects together. He and his wife helped us lay down a new roof for our carport and we helped them build and paint a shed in their back yard. Unfortunately, I chose a color for the shed that everyone else hated; it matched one of Stephen's ties. We ended up repainting the shed a different colour, amid much banter and laughter. On a more serious side of being and life, Stephen could always be counted on for various projects and emergencies. For instance, the time I was left holding a falling mulberry tree in the backyard. It was summer and all our windows were open, so I called out "Stephen, Stephen, help – the tree is falling over and I'm standing here holding it up. And it's heavy..." And I heard in the distance, "I'm commiinngg ...."

We often had discussions on the ego and its various traps, and the inner workings of the self and its world. One day Stephen quietly mentioned that he had investigated yoga and other disciplines of this nature when he was in his twenties. I offered to teach him how to meditate, and invited him to come to the philosophy classes and meditations held at my house. Stephen expressed a desire to learn meditation and to come to the classes, but somehow something, some activity or inner resistance, always seemed to intervene.

After living next door for a few activity-filled years, Stephen's life and marriage began to unravel. We would sometimes meet outside, by his front garden. Even though still soft-spoken, I could see the depth of his inner turmoil and struggle. His almost unlined, young face seemed uncharacteristically furrowed and serious, as though he were now grappling with untried and difficult emotions for the first time – almost like a child still too innocent to comprehend the disappointments and inevitable pain of life. After some thought, I gave him a prayer to say –

50

the Mercy Prayer of St. Faustina. The coming Sunday was the Day of Mercy. I told him that Christ Himself had promised St. Faustina that whoever said this prayer at the Hour of Mercy each day, would have their prayers answered – if their request was good for their souls and the souls of others. The Day of Mercy came only once a year, and certainly his prayers would be answered if he prayed on that day. He thanked me, and I later learned that Stephen had prayed and meditated in his own fashion, that Sunday afternoon.

Some months later Stephen found a very special woman. And one day in the garden, he told me that they planned to marry within the year. I rarely saw him now, for he had moved some towns away. The last time I saw him, his last words to me were : "I've never been so happy," and he smiled his quiet, young smile. He was full of hope for the future and the joy of his new life, when he was suddenly and tragically, from our point of view – called to other realms.

This struck others as a senseless tragedy, a young man of such vitality and worth suddenly taken away by a rare and fatal illness. In this case, I was more happy for my friend Stephen than sad at my own loss, because I knew that he would immediately go to a very high realm.

A few days after Stephen's death I was standing in the living room, on my way to the kitchen, when Stephen appeared to me in the woodpile by the coal stove. He was very transparent, mainly Light. I could barely make out his form. He was speaking very quietly and earnestly, and he said he was sorry that he had not come to our meditation and philosophy classes while he was on Earth. He said, "I wasn't ready." And then after a few more words that I could not hear, he disappeared.

His apology was very unexpected and surprising. His not coming to classes seemed like such a small thing, and certainly nothing to apologize for.

Some years later, in Earth time, I was looking at a photograph of Stephen that his ex-wife had given me, which I keep on the music rack of the upright piano in the living room. It was a large photograph of Stephen at a pumpkin farm, pulling a little wagon full of pumpkins and dried corn, looking into the camera with such a sweet and unguarded expression. That night, when I looked at the photograph, he gave me a big, radiant smile – and I was inwardly led to understand that he had recently been told that he would soon be transitioned to an even higher realm. I looked inside and found the realm, and it was a beautiful one. I smiled back and sent him my Love – and my best wishes for the journey.

Intelligent and articulate, attractive and spiritual – my friend Leslie was a beautiful person and carried much Light. When I think of her, the image of her smiling and laughing first comes to mind, and that image hangs, lingers there now, even as I write this.

In our many interactions over the years, I learned to admire and respect her. I always enjoyed Leslie's ready wit, and her incisive observation of life and its events and meanings and those who participate in the seemingly endless intertwinings of destiny and desire that we call life. If one could imagine a person who lived a complex yet simple life simultaneously, a person who could be both serious and fun-loving, who ran through life like a speeding bullet and yet loved stillness – then one might be thinking of Leslie. My last meeting with her on Earth was in Woolworth's parking lot, looking at flowers. And my last memory of her is a radiant smile.

Leslie "died" while in her mid-forties, after a long illness. I was still too injured to visit with her, but towards the end of her last illness I sent her a large vase filled with bright and summer-coloured flowers. My last verbal message from Leslie was a grateful "thank you" for the bouquet.

Until I met her in the garden, a few days after she left for other realms.

She was standing in the holly bush near my piano studio – well, our visitors from other realms are unembodied, and on another vibrational level, they don't need to be careful of where they stand – Stephen actually appeared in the woodpile near the coal stove. And my friend Leslie was very, very transparent, mainly Light; I could just barely make out her form. She was speaking to me, and I could hear her, but it was not clairaudient – the sound was not outside myself, nor was it an inner voice. I was hearing her speak in her own realm, and she was apologizing for something insignificant that she had said or done. It was so insignificant, that now I cannot remember what she said, only that it was an apology.

I do remember being very surprised, and wondering why she had come to see me in this way. I would not have been surprised had she appeared in the holly bush and told me all about her realm, whom she had seen, what she had done – or if she had just come to say 'hello' and had watched me work in the garden.

Up until these two meetings with Stephen and Leslie, which followed each other fairly closely in our Earth time/space frame, I assumed that when we left for other realms – we left for those realms with a new perspective and a new, better understanding of our earthly existence – and then thought no more about it, we moved onward and upward.

It had not occurred to me that we would first revisit our friends – or I suppose enemies, if we have them – on Earth, and try to make our reparations here.

I was very touched by both these meetings. From our earthly view, at least from my earthly view, neither of these apologies was necessary.

It showed me how transparent those realms are,
and that what is expected of us there is far
beyond the expectations and natural abilities
of earthly existence – unless one is
perhaps a saint.

So much is hidden from our view here, even our inner view is so clouded and veiled. Transparency while still on Earth is not an easy thing to achieve, perhaps an impossibility. But these two meetings instilled in me the wish and intent – and the means – to at least try.

My Teacher George King Driscoll

My decision to become a concert pianist was made at the age of five and a half years old, while my best friend, Ellen Dubin, wearing a beautiful white dress, played "Night Train" in her first piano recital. I hadn't even had my first lesson. I began piano lessons a few weeks later, with the woman who lived next door to us. When I was seven years old, my parents bought an upright piano for me to practice on and found me another teacher. When I was in the fourth grade, my mother came home from a meeting with my schoolteacher and said I could add on another instrument if I wished. I chose clarinet. To be honest, I wanted to play like Benny Goodman. By the age of fourteen or fifteen, I was playing clarinet professionally, in various classical orchestras.

My personal goal in high school was to one day join a major orchestra, and live the life of a professional musician. Towards this end, I applied to the Eastman School of Music and auditioned for them, on clarinet. For the needed recommendation, I approached the superintendent of music at my high school. He misheard my request and sent the recommendation to Ithaca College instead. A year later I arrived, unwilling and unhappy, at Ithaca College as a clarinet major.

Toward the end of my freshman year, someone came by my dormitory room and asked if I wanted to hear Professor Driscoll's piano concert. He was the best piano professor on the faculty and he rarely gave concerts. This was an opportunity one should not miss. For whatever reason – everything is a bit hazy, including the person who asked me to the concert and the reasons I went – I agreed to go.

I can remember that night as though it were yesterday. As a young professional clarinetist, I had played with some of the finest musicians of our day – famous conductors, first chair players of the New York Philharmonic, members of the National Symphony, famous composers. As a pianist I had studied with more than one teacher who had toured and given concerts in major concert halls. But nothing compared to what I heard that night from Professor Driscoll. I had never heard anything like his playing, not in concert and not on recording. His playing was extraordinary and electrifying. The concert imprinted itself so deeply on my mind, that over thirty years later when I took out the score to one of the pieces on his programme – Feu d'Artifice by Claude Debussy – I remembered every note of the piece and how he had interpreted those notes. I could hear the sounds and I could see his hands and fingers as he played – as though I were onstage with him as he played.

I had been listening to the great piano literature since I was five years old, with certain images in my mind of what piano playing was, what music was.

Simply stated, Driscoll's concert turned my musical world upside down. He showed me a new world, a whole new concept of the art of playing the piano and music in general. I wanted to live where he was living inwardly and share in his vision. I wanted to be a true musician.

The next day, I resolutely knocked on Driscoll's studio door and asked if I could audition for him. He politely asked me in to his studio, and smiled when I said that I was a clarinet major. Since I had brought no music with me, he put some of his scores on the piano rack for me to sight-read through. Unlike Rubinstein – Driscoll readily accepted me as his pupil.[10]

George was tall, very thin and dignified, with a lined, chiseled face that had something of an Irish priest in it. He seemed very, very old to me – although he was probably only in his late fifties. He spoke quietly and chose his words carefully, whether it was during lessons or class or while telling a personal tale – which he often did – and he had a way of looking inward when speaking and thinking about music or important events or people in his life. He also had a way of stressing certain words in a sentence in order to bring them into relief, and used pauses and various rhythms to better underline the meaning he wished to convey. Even though his speech was gentle and often restrained, disciplined – his laughter was hearty and loud by comparison, sounding remarkably like "ho, ho, ho"– a style we students endlessly imitated when left to ourselves.

George had always lived alone, at least in all the years I knew him, and he had the sensitivity and introspection that living alone can bring. In lessons or in repertory classes he said very little – but the words he chose always seemed to find the underlying problem. A student might play an entire movement from a Mozart Sonata or from a Classical or Romantic Concerto very chaotically or with no expression, and afterwards professor Driscoll would go over to the piano and respectfully say: "Hold the dotted quarter note longer, you are rushing it, you see" – and he would play one short passage for the class. When the student ran through the piece for the second time, using the corrected rhythmic motive – the interpretation and phrasing, as well as the deeper meaning of the piece would easily fall into place, both for those of us listening and for the person who had just played. It is not surprising that Driscoll corrected a badly played rhythmic motive. What was highly unusual was that he determined that the rhythm was the real problem, and limited his correction to that one fault out of so many, sometimes countless, others.

This is quite different from how most teachers teach, well-meaning teachers who give the student a hundred different corrections in one lesson – which leaves the student baffled and thinking more about the corrections than the

---

[10] *In my "dream" about Rubinstein.*

music itself. George King, as we often called him among ourselves, used to always remind us: "Your relationship is with the music and the piano, not with me." Basically, he handed us ourselves in those lessons, forcing us to develop our own varied and individual styles within the confines of the written score and intentions of the composer.

In lessons or in class, Driscoll would often lean forward in his chair, listening so intently one might think that he himself was playing every note. Often, in private lessons, he would play along on the second piano – he had a tremendous repertoire and was an extraordinary sight-reader. Or he would walk over to one piano and play a few phrases of the music with such Beauty and clarity that the rest of us could only wonder if one day, we too could perhaps come close to such mastery. For the sounds that emerged from the piano in those few measures or notes, seemed to bring with them the essence of the music and the composer's intent. George was a true musician. By the time I knew him he rarely gave concerts, but I always felt he was one of the greatest pianists of our age. Many years later, playing at his home, I would tease him and say, "If you don't give more concerts, They will send you back to Earth as a pianist, you'll have to do this all over again in another life," and he would playfully reply "I wouldn't mind that," and he would laugh in his energetic and happy way.

George King often held the repertory classes for his graduate piano students at his home. A handful of students would arrive in the early evening, sometimes on the coldest of winter nights, with the temperature outside below zero Fahrenheit. Often we played well into the night – solo pieces almost ready for a concert, or Concertos on two pianos, with one student playing the piano solo while the other read a transcription of the orchestra part on the other piano. Or four of us would sight-read transcriptions of Beethoven Symphonies or other compositions arranged for eight hands, with two students at each piano. These master classes I attended with great anticipation and joy – and I suspect his other students felt the same; the snow and noisy, biting wind was left outside in the night, and the warmth of the music and our common ideals and camaraderie filled his rooms as we played or listened to our classmates.

Two beautiful Steinway grand pianos stood majestically side by side in the living room, always polished and dusted, and music scores from his vast library were either neatly stacked near a piano or carefully filed away in another room. A pencil drawing of Rachmaninov hung on one wall, and a portrait of George as a young man, done in oils by a friend, faced you as you sat at the pianos. A framed photograph of his own master teacher stared down from another wall. One afternoon, after I had completed all my studies at the college and received my Master's degree, he pointed to the photograph and said, "He is my father and you are the grandchild." In the more than thirty years that I knew him, this was perhaps the most personal comment he ever made about our relationship. Once I sent him a letter while I was on vacation from school in my first year of study, and he answered it. Twenty years later he mailed me a postcard from Europe. We had never met outside of the college and its studios and concert halls, or his home, not in all the years I knew him. Yet we expressed our love and respect for each other in a thousand ways, in a gesture, a tone of voice, a smile, in my endless hours of piano practice to please him, his years of free lessons after I had graduated from the college, by a glance or a vase of flowers for his table – but never openly, and never verbally.

The many large windows in Driscoll's house had light, semi-transparent curtains, and all the rooms were a Dover white or cream colour, and simply furnished. Here and there oriental rugs in thin, worn strips covered the bare hardwood floors. Plants of various sizes, shapes and ages stood in the windows and on the coffee table by the tan-coloured, textured couch George always sat on. The two armchairs were of a similar tan colour and texture - and the feeling of the house was one of openness and light which one sometimes finds in old houses. It also reflected the basic sunny optimism of George's life, which contrasted in an unusual and interesting way with the depth and intensity of his playing and inmost feelings. In addition to his natural optimism, he showed an almost childlike delight in the beauty of life around him: in the small shamrock plant someone had recently given him, or the birch trees in the yard – or the scrawny clematis that was winding itself slowly and painstakingly around a tree trunk in the shaded back garden. George would point to these various miracles with pride, as if to say: "Life is so wondrous, isn't it?" which I found to be the same attitude he brought to every note of every score he played or taught.

For lessons or classes at his home, one always rang the lower front bell, which was labeled George King Driscoll. If you peeked through the curtains on the door, you could almost make out George opening the inner door and coming through the small, narrow hallway to open the front door. He always greeted you with a big smile and a happy "Come in, and follow me," and led you back to the living room. "What do you have for me today?" he would say, and often he would first go to the piano and show you what he himself had been working on that morning. In the years that he taught at the college he would arise at five a.m., in order to practice for some hours before his teaching day began. On one visit to see him, he was now in his seventies, he brought me to the piano and showed me the score to a Debussy piece he had read through that morning, and he spoke about it as most people speak of their children, with such delight and pleasure at its beauty and workmanship. He was on his knees before the entire piano literature, and the only time I saw him angry with a student was when he thought they had not taken their study of a piece, or the piece itself, seriously. Then he could be like a tiger protecting her cub. I only saw this twice in all the years I knew him – but I'm sure no one in the room ever forgot the experience.

One day while still a student at the college, I asked Driscoll which Chopin

Etude I should study next, and without hesitation he replied : "All of them."
I took him seriously, of course, and began to study more of them, adding a
few to my repertoire each year. He himself, I'm sure, had studied them all.

When he played them with me in lessons, on the second piano, they were -
effortless. Effortless. The thirds etude, which most professional pianists
would never attempt in concert – sounded like the wind blowing across the
sea, or leaves wafting off into the distance on a sunny day when he played it.
The more intense etudes sounded as though inner bells had been written
into the score, with thousands of other notes articulated clearly yet sub-
servient to the main and inner melodies, producing waves of harmonies,
which magically arose as though emerging from the music and the piano
without human intervention. Sometimes I would stand by the piano watching and listening - and when he had finished I would simply inwardly groan
and say: "How in the world did you do that?" And George would slowly
stand up from the piano bench and laugh his wonderful laugh.

George, both the person and the musician, radiated brilliant white Light.
One afternoon he told me an interesting story from his youth. A visiting psychic had come to town, not an unusual occurrence in those days, and
George decided to go to his public "psychic show." During the performance, the hall was partially darkened and the clairvoyant answered questions
from the audience and gave psychic readings. At one point a man seated
directly behind George King asked the showman a few questions, and the
psychic replied: "I can't answer you because I can't see you. The young gentleman seated in front of you has too much Light; his Light is obscuring my
view of you." That young man was George. He was no stranger to the mystical life. One day I came in for a lesson and he asked me if I smelled per-
fume. There was a lingering scent of violets, and I asked him who had been
there. George looked at me and quietly said "No one of this world."

Those wonderful afternoons, when George would tell story after story in the
parlor. And then: "Well, that's enough. Let's play some music," – and we
would go to the pianos, where he had carefully arranged some scores for us
to read through that day. One morning I brought the score to Mahler's Fifth
Symphony, arranged for four hands. We played and played and finally
George said, "Let's stop, I'm getting tired." His eyesight was weakening
with age, and the score to Mahler's Fifth was difficult and exhausting even
with perfect eyesight. Disappointed, I said "How old are you?" And he
answered "Seventy-two." I looked at the page number and said, "Well, we
are on page seventy-one. Let's do one more page for your age and an extra
one or two for good luck." He laughed, and we dove back in for a few more
pages.

Even after I had completed my studies at the college, George and I played
or read through Symphonies or other works for four hands or two pianos
several times a week, and for many years after I had finished my formal stud-

ies with him. After each session, he would ask when I wished to come again, and we would either set a time for our next meeting or call each other impromptu. One Easter Sunday George telephoned and said in his familiar way, "It's Easter Sunday. Let's celebrate. Can you come over and play duets?" I walked to his house, which was then only a block or two away from mine. He had lined up many symphonic scores for us to play through, and as he opened each book he would explain why he had chosen it. And as we both sat there together at the piano, I would see the two of us sight-reading the scores, as though from a great distance – the thin young woman and the tall, frail old gentleman, side by side on the polished music bench, beautiful clouds and textures and landscapes of music arising from the piano – as though I were watching and enjoying the spectacle before me from another realm.

Shortly after my young and talented piano student Alyssa "died," I went to visit with George. He was in the back garden when I arrived, seated in a lawn chair. I sat down beside him and marveled at the tremendous Light and Divine Presence that was in the garden that day. The Light was crystalline, and right in front of us. There was so much Light that I could not discern a form, although it was wonderful to just look at the Light.

Later Driscoll said that he had seen Christ in the garden that day.

Not long before George left for other realms, my friend Joan took me to visit him for the last time. They had been close friends long before I met either of them. In fact, Driscoll had been Joan's theory teacher at Ithaca College, and later they both were on the faculty. He was now very old, and as we spoke and drank cups of coffee with sugared biscuits I learned that he could no longer teach or play the piano, his hands now gnarled and twisted as they rested on the kitchen table. Because of my injuries, I had not been able to see him for many years, and I was not prepared for what I perceived and heard that afternoon. Before we said good bye, for the first and only time in our long and deep life together, I impulsively went over and embraced him. Still the Titan in terms of presence and inner life, he was so thin and insubstantial physically, it was almost as though I were embracing air. I stood by the door and turned to him – because our relationship had always been so reserved and outwardly polite, I was worried that I might have overstepped an emotional or professional boundary. Instead, he looked at me and said simply "Thank you."[11]

After our visit, Joan and I both commented on how frail George looked, and our remaining discussion on the way home pivoted on this discouraging fact. I was concerned enough that I mentioned him in my next letter to my friend Sister Mary Magdalene, a nun in a Carmelite monastery at Greystones, Ireland, and asked her to pray for him.

Years earlier, Driscoll had told me of a recurring sort of dream that he had.

In these dreams he was a Carmelite monk, living a simple, prayerful life in an old stone monastery in Ireland with other Carmelite monks. He said that in his latest dream about his life in the monastery, a bishop had come to visit them. Because of various troubles and complaints in other religious houses, the bishop had been sent to change the rule of the monastery to an easier one. However, on inspecting the monks and the monastery, he was so pleased with their lives and spiritual achievement that he had decided not to change their laws or vows. And as George related this dream to me – what struck me most was not the dream, but how seriously he seemed to believe in it. He looked so very pleased and delighted that the bishop had not changed the rule – as though he truly did live in that monastery as a monk.

Sister Mary Magdalene wrote back to me, saying that she was praying for my teacher. She enclosed a scapular for him, carefully folded between the sheets of her letter.[12]

Because of my injuries I was still not able to walk into town, nor drive a car. I put the scapular sent from Sr. Mary in an envelope and mailed it to George. I also enclosed a short note that said something to the effect of: "This scapular is from Sr. Mary Magdalene in Ireland, who is a Carmelite nun. And if anything happens to you, please make sure that you are wearing it." A week later George's nephew, Patrick, called me to tell me that George had passed away the night before.[13]

I later mused about the scapular sent by Sister Mary and concluded that Our Lady must have truly wanted George to have Her scapular, to have one sent all the way from Ireland. On deeper reflection, it became more extraordinary in light of his recurrent dreams about his life in the Carmelite

---

[11] *As I write this, I remember that many times, after playing a long and difficult Chopin Rhapsody or Scherzo, or a Beethoven Sonata, Driscoll would wordlessly stand when I had finished and also simply and quietly say those same words. "Thank you." Conservatory students are prepared for and expecting to hear many corrections and suggestions during lessons. To have a professor thank a student for playing - is generally unheard of. Driscoll's respect for his students' personal interpretation of music as an expression of their being and soul, allowed him to impart a dignity and inner conviction to their playing. This quality was also a testimony to Driscoll's great love for music, for he had undoubtedly heard countless other students' work on that same piece, countless times, and in various stages and states of excellence or disrepair.*

[12] *The scapular represents our devotion to the Madonna. It also symbolizes that we are wearing Her vestment, i.e. the Carmelite habit. It is said that the first scapular appeared miraculously in the hands of the Carmelite monk St. Simon Stock. It is promised that those who wear the scapular at the hour of death will not suffer eternal punishment. Moreover, the Madonna has promised that anyone who wears the scapular at the moment of death will be taken to Heaven by Her personally.*

monastery. There suddenly seemed to exist an interesting mystical relationship between Driscoll, Sister Mary Magdalene, myself and the scapular.[14] Was this to validate that yes, on a deep level of his being, George had been a monk in that Carmelite monastery in Ireland? To compound the irony, I had at least a hundred scapulars in my upstairs middle room. I had never thought to give him one – although I give scapulars away all the time, often to people I barely know, for the protection and graces they give us in our daily lives. The mysterious workings of the Divine in our lives are not always this easy to see. But they are there. Even my first meeting with Driscoll was the careful arrangement of apparent mistakes and coincidences.

To end this story, I should say that although I have written the news of George King's "death" very calmly, my reaction at the time was not so philosophic. After I finished speaking with Patrick, I telephoned my friend JF. She and I had been in college together, and she knew perhaps better than anyone what Driscoll meant to me both as a teacher and as a friend throughout the years. When JF arrived at my house I was crying bitterly, and she offered to give me a short massage, undoubtedly to comfort me and to calm me down. As she arranged cushions on the bare wood floor, so that I could rest comfortably near the coal stove – she accidentally kicked the coal bucket, which made a terrible racket. Knowing that I am very sensitive to sound, she quickly straightened up and said, "Oh! I'm so sorry, I kicked the bucket!" And then she slowly started to laugh, and soon I joined in – because that is exactly what George would have said. Followed by his familiar "ho, ho, ho."[15]

---

13 *I hadn't even known that he was ill, nor consciously accepted the fact that he might be dying.*

14 *Sister Mary Magdalene died about six months after Driscoll.*

15 *George had so much Light when he was incarnate, it is not always possible to know when he is visiting, to clairvoyantly see him. Shortly after his death, I would see him sitting at the kitchen table or standing near the piano in the living room. But I have often felt his loving presence, and know that we will meet again in other realms.*

My Friend Joan

Joan was teaching trumpet and brass classes in the music school at Ithaca College, when I first met her. I was just eighteen years old.

I liked Joan instantly. Medium height and moderately thin, with somewhat short, cropped brown hair and angular features – Joan had an imposing presence, an innate dignity and natural authority for all her somewhat bohemian appearance.

Nine or so years after I graduated from college, Joan became the first conductor of the Ithaca Community Band; she asked me if I would play first chair clarinet. Astonished, I said: "I haven't played clarinet in over ten years." She said: "Just come." The qualities I had so admired in her classes soon applied to Joan, the conductor – and then to our growing friendship. I found her loyal and truthful, humble, and extremely intelligent and knowledgeable on many subjects. And an extraordinary musician. She had piercing brown eyes, and they were set in a way that often gave her a sad expression. I must have mentally traced the lines of Joan's face, her features and the structure of her face, innumerable, uncountable times. Those memories have now partly faded, but not her eyes. It is her voice and her eyes that I remember most. And as the years go by, without seeing her across the table from me, or seated next to me, those two attributes seem to gain rather than lessen in intensity and memory.

She was happiest when in Nature – walking in the woods, or working in her gardens. Joan had grown up on Long Island, and her stories from that portion of her history seemed most joyful when she spoke about the sea. After her husband died, she led an almost monk-like existence. She practiced trumpet faithfully and diligently each day, had a few private students, worked for some hours in the gardens during those seasons, had her daily forty-five-minute nap and her early-morning walk. Evenings she went to orchestra or chamber rehearsals, played concerts, or visited with friends. For the last six or seven years of her life, every Saturday night she played Scrabble with the same friend.[16] Joan usually lost.

Joan and I had lunch or dinner together once or twice each week for almost twenty years, including the week before she died. I looked forward to those times together, for I loved to follow her interesting mind

---

[16] *This Scrabble friend, my teacher Driscoll, Joan and my little black cat Franz all "died" within a few weeks of each other.*

and its thoughts, and the way in which those thoughts formed and expressed themselves.

She would open with "Hi Laur" – Joan was one of the very small number of people who have ever called me that – and say: "I have some questions for you." She was extremely inquisitive and curious about people and life in general, and she usually brought a list of questions with her, written in a little notebook. These questions asked my opinion on a wide range of subjects, some personal, some musical, some philosophical and some factual; and some on unexpected and surprising topics like sea urchins or brands of paper clips, or where we bought our coal (she did not have a coal stove). Occasionally she brought the Sunday New York Times crossword puzzle, and we would work on some missing squares together.

Joan's wonderful sense of humor combined with the truthfulness of her statements, often left me speechless. Laughter was a large dimension of our times together. But it was a restrained laughter, laughter that was the result of her detached overview of a situation rather than humor for its own sake – a creative and intelligent humor that can connect people to themselves, to each other and to truth. She was one of the most rational people I have ever known, and one of the few I have ever relied on for advice. Her descriptions of events and people were always very incisive and to the point – she was not one to waste words or thoughts. She would carefully think before she answered in the low, calm voice that I so loved. Some piece of practical and sound advice usually followed. It was a remarkably balanced and mature relationship, based on mutual love and respect.

Joan never hesitated to declare that she did not believe in miracles – even though I was seeing them almost daily, and a good deal of my discussion was about them. Once, however, she did mention that she believed that people could be angels for each other. And when I spoke about the soul, she never contradicted me. In fact, she seemed to take great interest in our discussions on these topics. Yet, in all the time I knew her – which was over thirty years – she never spoke of her religious beliefs, she refused to divulge them.

One night, on the car ride back from dinner, Joan announced that the doctors had found a suspicious spot on her lung. She had the needed surgery and radiation treatment, and was in good spirits, but I did not have a good feeling about her apparent recovery. One Monday night about a year later, Joan said: "The pain in my shoulder is worse. I can't sleep at night." We were at dinner. It was now almost thirty-five years since my trumpet lessons with her at Ithaca College. Her deep brown eyes reflected her disquiet and some fear. "The doctor gave me these," and she gently placed a little orange plastic bottle filled with small, round white pills on the table between us. Morphine. Her fingers rested on the little vial for some moments and then she took her hand away, leaving the small plastic vial alone on the empty table, like a small, fragile tower or tiny pillar, all that stood between her and excruciating pain." He says the cancer has returned. I am scheduled to begin chemo next week. He says that with chemo I might have two years left."

The following Tuesday, I visited Joan in her hospital room and brought some flowers from the garden that I had hastily stuck in a vase. I asked how she was feeling. "They did tests, and now the doctor says that with chemotherapy I could maybe have two more months." I sat in the little metal chair next to her bed, staring at her with unbelief. Then she added: "I decided not to have the chemo. I have two or so more days." I sat there unmoving and said to myself – "From two years to two months – to two days. Just like that." I asked her if she wanted me to stay with her, in the hospital. She said, "Yes." Then she said: "Are you comfortable?" That was pretty much the last coherent conversation we had on earth. By that Thursday night – she was "gone." It was a helpless feeling, to be a Divine Healer and not be allowed to heal her – nor even appreciably ease her pain. A part of me was devastated.

As I walked out of the hospital parking lot with one of Joan's daughters, a little movie began playing in my head. I walked into the movie, and there was Joan. She was walking down a path cut through a field and walking towards a beautiful woods. It was early autumn, leaves were still on the trees, just turning colours, and she was wearing a light jacket and slacks. As she approached the woods, she turned to me and waved happily. She shouted something to me, but I couldn't hear her. She cupped her hands to her mouth and shouted something again, something that I still couldn't hear. So she smiled and waved again, and then turned and began walking into the beautiful woods. The scene floated farther and farther away, and then disappeared.

For weeks afterwards I kept hearing her voice, here and there, saying "Hi Laur," in that particular inflection and pronunciation that she had. And I continue to check in on her clairvoyantly, as I do with all my dear friends – if I am allowed.

I still miss her terribly, in spite of the fact that I can check up on her when I wish. Clairvoyance cannot always make up for even one run-of-the-mill conversation over a nice dinner.

Eleanor. One would be truly hard-pressed to describe my friend Eleanor, or her life. To choose from thousands of special thoughts, images, sentences, words, fragments of scenes and moments seems like a hopeless task. Yet I hear myself say "one must begin." One of Eleanor's favorite expressions was, "And then I heard myself say"....

More than twenty five years my senior, Eleanor was in many ways more youthful than I. In the last years, when she became more frail, she would say: "Sometimes I look down at this old body, and I can't believe it's me!" Physically, she had the rare sort of beauty that might make some people smile in appreciation, and others leave their wives, or at least turn back for another look. Clairvoyantly speaking – she had tremendous, radiant Light. Her radiance at times – was breathtaking.

In terms of personality, Eleanor could be innocently charming and gay. She had a wonderful lightness of being – and a great wit, and the natural intelligence that makes such humor possible. She would say, "I look so conventional on the outside. If people only knew!" and she would laugh in her silvery way and say, "O Laur".... Loving, artistic – with a rare gentleness and understanding of life and people that one cannot put into a few words on an empty page. Let me just say that in the twenty five or more years that I knew her, I never heard her say a negative word about any other creature on this earth, human or otherwise.

Our Love – as with the others mentioned in this book - is very special and deep, and more than just a human friendship. It is the manifested, conscious Love of one soul to another soul, the Divine Love – and thus Eternal.

Eleanor, throughout her life, had the varied life experiences that matched the many different facets of her personality. Her lightness of being – although wonderful to be around, like being near a beautiful, fluttering butterfly – was not always to her advantage. What comes to mind tonight as I write this, is the time I grabbed the steering wheel of her car while I was in dream state. This saved her from driving her car into a meadow on the way into town (there is not much to tell; in the "dream" Eleanor was driving her car along a country road and did not see the sharp turn directly ahead of her –from above and behind her, I lunged at the steering wheel and turned it for her. I saw the surrounding fields and colours very clearly, but my only thought was to turn the steering wheel hard and quickly to the right. I only zoomed in for this short episode and then went back to my normal dreamless sleep).

Eleanor was an absolutely terrible driver, (one of her sons eventually prohibited any of his children or grandchildren from riding in a car she was driving) for the simple reason that she could barely keep her mind on the road. In the instance above – she was coming into town to pay me a surprise visit – and as she later explained, she saw a wondrous bird and forgot that she was driving a car. "And then somehow the steering wheel turned all on its own, and kept me from going off the road into a field," she said happily when she arrived at my house.

"I turned the wheel for you," I replied, and added : "Try to remember where you are and what you're doing, because next time I might be busy doing something else." She stared at me for a moment and then said "Oh – you turned the wheel. Thank you!"

That was one side of Eleanor.

Dignified and profound was another side, leonine and regal – one could find a beautiful Spanish Contessa if one looked hard enough. And laughter, childlike laughter echoes throughout my memories of her, woven through the so many moments and years we shared, with Light and magic everywhere we went – for she carried many angels with her. I can see her now, simply but beautifully dressed, always surrounded by Light, in pale or striking earth tone colours, sometimes with a bright splash, depending on her mood – and holding a natural elegance that one is either born with, or otherwise strives unsuccessfully to acquire.

I also see her sitting silently in meditation, across from me on cushions, her beautiful face lit by a slight smile. In spite of her deceptively ordinary appearance, she was no stranger to Mystical experience. She also had some clairvoyance, with glimpses of the future – events foretold years in advance – flashing across her mind in vivid colours.

Eleanor had loved her husband and her children almost to adoration – so many of her stories were of her children when they were small and clinging to her skirts, or when they took up a new instrument at school, or when they brought their future wives home for the first time. And when she spoke of her husband and her life with him – I always felt as though I were there with her, her memories were so deep and alive. After her husband's death, Eleanor single-mindedly entered on the spiritual path – the Quest, as Paul Brunton calls it. She never doubted her decision. She never looked back. Entering on the Quest meant, in a certain real sense, giving up her personal wishes and dreams. Philosophic study and meditation replaced her duties as a housewife and mother, and gave her a new depth of being as well as a new vocabulary for the innate knowing she already possessed. Her inner being and attainment qualified her to become a teacher for many, yet she cloaked her wisdom in a gentle and grandmotherly manner of relating to those who came to her. Even though Eleanor held low-paying, fairly ordinary and unglamorous jobs in the outer world – a large part of the continued unfolding of her spiritual life was to guide and teach others.[17] This concern for others and her ability and willingness to guide them continued, even into her final weeks here on earth.

Eleanor's path was therefore filled with not only family, but also strangers and friends, some lost and asking directions, or needing companionship for some miles, or waving as they passed, or at an intersection. If they were crying in despair by the side of the road, she would stop and bring a comforting story or some home-baked bread or soup or a smile and some wise words. She would prod those walking too slowly, and if someone had stumbled, she would lend them her arm and her company – and her Light lit the path for many. Every person she met on this path - was equally important to her, because she looked deeply into and related to the person's soul, she looked past their appearance and their personality, directly into the Beauty and Vastness of their soul.

Alone and yet surrounded by people. Alone and merged with the soul – that might best describe Eleanor. She was like the Crystal shining in the sun, or submerged in water, when its colours are deepest and most vibrant – and one had to stand with her, submerged in the soul, the water, to truly see her Beauty – because she was not of this world, her thoughts and her Heart were truly Elsewhere. The Light she radiated and the Light she reflected cannot be seen if one is standing only in the world.

My last meeting with Eleanor was a few short hours before she died. She could no longer speak with words, but she turned her head on the pillow to look at me and gazed and gazed into my eyes, trusting my clairvoyance to tell me what she could not speak, the love and longing and regret, and hope of seeing one another all in that single gaze. I smiled and gave her a slow, single wave of benediction and Peace, a temporary adieu in return.

Hours later, in a small simple room, Eleanor's frail body took its last breath, rhythmically and with the precision of life's ordered existence. Those left in the room each grieved in their own way, and I went into another room and laid down on a stray couch I found there. I already missed her deeply. I closed my eyes – and within seconds there was my dear friend Eleanor. Radiant, dressed in a gown of light material, laughing – and dancing. Dancing with a man I couldn't clearly see, although

---

[17] *After she retired, she lived at Wisdom's Goldenrod and acted as overseer there until her death.*

67

I could discern that he was wearing a dark suit.[18] I assume that this man was her husband, a man whom she had thought and spoken about with such loyalty and steady love throughout the many years of our friendship.

As I lay there, torn between the temporary emptiness and disarray of our parting and the joyous pages of my dear Eleanor's new life in another realm – I smiled and wept simultaneously.

My adjustment to Eleanor's new form took only a few months – well, she was mainly Light while on Earth, it was not a difficult task. It has become a familiar thing, walking down the street with her, meeting in various places in a fleeting and wonderful way, having conversations of sorts. I am not often clairaudient, so it is more an inner dialogue and inner response; often I just talk to her aloud, trusting that she can hear me. If not, she knows that I know she is there, which is the important thing.

About a month ago I felt Eleanor's presence, and when I clairvoyantly found her I realized that she was on her way to see my father, in another realm.

Eleanor had never known my father in this reality. She knew of my love for him, however. And even though I do not fully understand why she went to see him – although she was a curious person while on earth, I doubt that she undertook the journey simply out of curiosity – I do know that the reasons were somehow tied to her love and concern for me.

I saw that realm from a distance, and it was exceedingly beautiful and bright and I felt the Light and clarity of their meeting. There was so much Light, I could not see clearly and the images were indistinct and very transparent. I was not allowed to enter, nor accompany Eleanor consciously. However, I was there on some level of my being the entire afternoon, half in this realm and half in that realm. It was as though I were near the sea, a beautiful expanse of sea and radiant sun and crystalline air.

Even now I can inwardly catch a glimpse of where we were that day, and the joy and clarity of that realm – and the depth and wonder of that meeting.

---

[18] *One of Eleanor's sons read this story and commented that Eleanor herself had seen the same vision, years earlier.*

Jeremy

I first met Jeremy at the checkout counter of the old Woolworth's. Jeremy was at the head of our line, and he looked about seven years old. He was fairly small and slight, and he was wearing a thin fall jacket and long pants. His little brother Justin's feet were a few inches from my right elbow. He was ensconced in the front basket of his mother's shopping cart, facing me.

I was in line behind them, and my shopping cart was filled with thirty or so honey-coloured teddy bears that were presents for poor children at Christmas. Justin had a few pale smudges of dirt on his face, and his little tan jacket was worn and dingy from wear. He could have been the poster child for the children I was buying presents for. He calmly and wordlessly watched me pile up the bears on the counter, maintaining an expressionless demeanor that only comes with remarkable self control. The stack of bears grew and continued to grow, and then spilled out over the counter under his elbow. I finally gave him one. He took it readily, with a shy, pale smile and big eyes, and his mother turned around and gently protested. Finally she said: "He already has bears at home," to which I replied, "Well, now he has another one," and I watched the three of them leave the store, Jeremy in the lead and Justin in the rear, still in the cart and still holding the bear with both hands.

A year or two later, a new young piano student came in for his first lesson, accompanied by his mother. As I welcomed them in, the mother looked around the living room and her eyes rested on a honey-coloured teddy bear who sat on a stack of music scores on a shelf behind the piano. I kept him there for moral support for all my students, including the adults. "You gave Justin the bear," she said – and I had no idea what this woman was saying, not until she reminded me of the scene at Woolworth's years earlier. We all thought it an interesting coincidence and probably also an auspicious start to Jeremy's lessons.

Jeremy was a musical genius – and probably one of the most difficult students I have ever worked with. He was still fairly small and thin, and had a beautiful face, not the sort of face one usually sees on a little boy – and wonderful blue eyes. He usually wore striped polo shirts and jeans to his lessons, although one day he came in proudly wearing a second-hand dark suit jacket. It was before his first concert, and he wore it with great panache and almost the casual dignity one would find in a world-famous composer or writer. He was home-schooled, as was his brother Justin, and they spent hours each day working in the family gardens. So, generally Jeremy came in for his lessons looking like a farmer's child, with mud or berries or grass clippings clinging to his shoes, if not all his clothing. And from all those hours in the fields and gardens, his hands and arms and back had developed tremendous strength and flexibility, and dexterity. Even as a young boy he was capable of a surprising, tremendous power and virtuosity at the keyboard.

When Jeremy first came to me, he had already studied for a year and some months with another teacher. He brought with him little Bach and Chopin pieces, which he raced through like a maniac, with his foot held on the sustaining pedal so long that basically it was all a big, blurry mass of trembling sound by the end of the piece.

I admired his enthusiasm and agility – but we had many discussions on rhythm and how to use the foot pedals in those initial lessons. His other teacher had taught him everything by rote or by ear, following the Suzuki method of teaching. Jeremy either had developed, or was born with perfect pitch – which means the person can identify every tone by its letter name. If I played an "A" on the piano – Jeremy could be in another room with his back towards the piano and could easily say "you just played an 'A'." For a musician – especially a pianist – this is a great gift. His first teacher had so successfully helped him to develop this gift that Jeremy eventually could hear a piece played once on the radio – and then go to the piano and play it. The great pianist/composer Alexander Scriabin also had this ability, as did Sergei Rachmaninov, I believe.

However, this method of teaching also meant that Jeremy had not learned to read notes off the written score. This deficiency was crippling him, and we had many discussions about it in that first year. Reading notes off the page is very difficult, especially for children who can barely read written words yet. Therefore, most children prefer to memorize or play by ear. Finally I said: "Jeremy. What are you going to do if someone asks you to sit down and play something new, a piece you haven't studied yet, at a party, or at an audition, or maybe even in concert? Are you going to say 'Excuse me for a few days while I listen to a recording of that piece over and over first.'" He laughed, but he began to take the art of note-reading seriously.

Worse than the above problems – which were all fairly easily solved – Jeremy was so sensitive to sound, timbre and pitch, that if a piano was not exactly and perfectly tuned – he could not play on it.

He would become so distracted and frustrated by the mis-tuning that he literally stopped playing in the middle of a phrase and could not continue. Frankly, I forget how we got through this problem, but somehow we did.

Aside from the above, I could say that Jeremy was the most gifted young student given to me, in all the years that I taught piano. Because he was being home schooled, he had many hours a day to practice, and the support and encouragement of those around him. His parents soon bought him a beautiful Mason and Hamlin grand piano to practice on, and endless recordings to listen to. He also had great natural gifts. Moreover, his first teacher had brought him to truly love and enjoy playing the piano. By the time Jeremy came to me to study, he had already been given an excellent foundation to build on, and was prepared and primed to be a great pianist. I then merely gave him the willingness to work and the tools to get there.

When Jeremy came in for lessons we always began with technique. Side by side on the piano bench, we started the complicated patterns slowly and then sped up later in each exercise. This was our compromise, for he wanted to race through everything – yet it is in the slow practice that we truly develop a sure technique. We transposed and played every pattern in all keys, sometimes in different rhythms and with different fingerings, for many octaves up and down the keyboard. I made sure that I outplayed him mightily in everything we did, otherwise he would no longer practice. Eventually I began to make up exercises for us to do, in order to keep him excited and interested: finger-twisters with thumbs on the black keys, or some other difficult task he had not yet tried. Soon he was inventing his own exercises and bringing them in for me to play, undoubtedly his good-natured attempt to find something I could not do.

He was an extraordinary child. Sometimes I wondered who was the student and who was the teacher. By the time he was nine years old we could spend hours together, discussing music and interpretations and various pianists. His comments were often quite astute. One day he telephoned to ask if we could discuss and analyze a unique, unpublished cadenza written by Vladimir Horowitz. The great pianist had written it for one of Franz Liszt's famous Hungarian Rhapsodies; Jeremy had found it on an old Horowitz recording remastered for compact disc. We had an exciting and enjoyable time, listening to the recording and then working together to untangle the blur of crashing and speeding notes. Jeremy had already figured out how to isolate and repeat only that portion of the disc – a feat I, even to this day, have never mastered. I must admit that I kept a copy of the cadenza for myself and have often played it in concert – something I would not have thought of doing on my own.

Within a year or two of lessons with me, Jeremy was studying the true piano literature, including Chopin Etudes, Mazurkas and Polonaises. He played Chopin's very famous Polonaise in A Major, Opus 40 Nr.1- up to tempo and at full volume on his first recital as my student. A friend of mine stopped in one day while Jeremy was playing the very difficult and celebrated left hand octave section of Chopin's Polonaise in

A flat major, Op. 53, up to tempo and with the clarity and precision and the full power of a grown man – the sound filling my house to the brim and overflowing to my yard and probably the street as well. Jeremy was still so physically small that my friend could not even see who was playing, his head was hidden by the music rack. It looked as though no one was playing the piece, until you looked down and saw his thin little leg and his sneakered foot working the sustaining pedal. My friend looked at me and looked at the piano, looked at me with amazement and then back to the piano in amazement – I am sure that was an experience she will not forget.

Jeremy once asked me what the most difficult piece ever written for piano was – and I told him that in my opinion, Chopin's Etude in thirds was probably the most difficult piece ever written – a piece he immediately began to study on his own. He seemed to thrive on challenges, in every area of his life.

Jeremy had now studied with me for several years, and was obviously headed for a wonderful career as a pianist – when I had my car accident and could no longer teach him. When I was well enough to speak on the phone, I advised all my students to find another teacher. I called Jeremy about every six months or so, and continued to encourage him to find another teacher. To my knowledge, he tried a teacher or two and then eventually gave up classical piano.

Jeremy and I called or saw each other only a few times over the next ten years. Until one night in my living room when he was twenty-two years old.

It was very late at night, I was almost ready to go upstairs. I was sitting on the couch with some papers in my hand when a conversation with Jeremy began in my mind. I knew it was Jeremy; it was his voice – but he sounded very, very far away. The words were so indistinct I was unable to make them out. I listened intently anyway, for this is not unusual, for the words to be too indistinct to consciously understand. His voice was serious and low, and as he continued speaking a little "movie" began in my head. I did not step into it until it became my entire world as I sometimes do, instead I closed my eyes and allowed it to continue to play as a movie against the screen of my mind. In this clairvoyant scene, which was in vivid colours, I saw Jeremy's house – and it was filled with people. People I did not recognize, and they were walking around the house, sitting, entering and leaving – I knew his parents and brothers were there, but I couldn't determine why all those people were in the house. As I watched this moving and changing scene I was also listening to Jeremy's distant and low voice. Jeremy spoke for a long time, it seemed for at least twenty minutes, and I was not at all pleased with what he was telling me, or what I was seeing. In fact, I was very annoyed, displeased. Towards the end of the clairvoyant vision, the initial scene dissolved and was replaced by a new series of quickly changing scenes and images. These images were less distinct, and always showed someone in Jeremy's family. I remember thinking to myself when it had ended, "I must call Jeremy tomorrow," and then I immediately fell asleep on the couch.

When I awoke the next morning, I remembered nothing of our conversation or the images I had seen the night before. The thought to call Jeremy crossed my mind briefly, but I quickly became distracted by my day and the thought vanished as quickly as it had arisen.

The following day – it was a Friday morning – I awoke to a phone message from Jeremy's mother Betty. Jeremy had been killed the night before, in a terrible car crash. She was crying on the phone, and I could hardly bear to hear her voice in such great pain. I did not know what to say to her so I decided to call her later in the day, when I was more awake and had had some time to think.

It was then that I remembered my clairvoyant vision and the conversation with Jeremy two days earlier. Interestingly enough – I still could not remember a word of our conversation.

There was no time to dwell on these memories however, because Jeremy was now standing right in front of me in the living room, talking a mile a minute and very excitedly – joyfully. He was so happy that he seemed almost crazed, like Daniel in the blue world of Light.

Only Jeremy was beyond the blue world – he was
all white Light. In fact, there was so much Light,
I could not see his form. I could only see his
Light. Although I could hear him speaking,
I could not understand a word he was saying.

And Jeremy – as in life – wouldn't stop talking.

He talked for hours that first day. By the time I called his mother back – well, it was now difficult to relate to her terrible grief when her son, the object of her agony, was standing next to me joyous and happy and radiant with Light and talking a blue streak. In my own way I tried to reassure her – but I could not come out and say: "Jeremy's here and he's fine and he loves you." We had never talked about my clairvoyance in the past, and I didn't think this was the time to bring it up. Over the

73

next days and weeks I did tell the family, and I also told them about the clairvoyant vision I had had a few nights before his accident.

Jeremy came for days, day after day. At this time I was preparing for a series of concerts, and it got to the point where I had to inwardly ask him to either stop talking or leave for a while so that I could practice. The concerts were all Robert Schumann, and Jeremy's energy at this time was more Chopinesque or Lisztian – in any case not Robert Schumann, with his sensitive and fragile clarity and the depth and seriousness of every note and every articulation exactly and impeccably placed within the phrase. I struggled through the last public concert, Jeremy's energy washing over me like a torrent in the gorge.

Over time, it has become clear to me – although I cannot say exactly how – that Jeremy told me that I was to write this book in those first days after he left this reality. I did not understand what he was saying at the time, for he was speaking in his own realm and I could not make out the specific words he was speaking, although I could inwardly hear the tone and rhythm of his words. I must admit that the book has progressed remarkably quickly and easily, several notebooks scribbled up within a few months or so, ideas and words pouring onto the page. People to be interviewed seemed to emerge from nowhere, with the perfect story to tell. Something tells me that Jeremy, in his great enthusiasm and boundless energy, has sent me many angels for this venture. And undoubtedly other friends, in other realms, have helped as well.

As a postscript – I was not the only person to see or communicate with Jeremy after he left his earthly body. Later, in the interview section of this volume, Jeremy's mother will speak of her own experiences with him after he left for other realms.

Visits with my Animal Friends
in Other Realms

SECTION

11

We always thought that White Cat was Nell's mother. They both adopted me when I was living on Black Road, in the country. Nell was a kitten, and White Cat – who showed up a bit after Lenny moved in as my housemate – was very white and fluffy and fully grown. I adopted Nell, and took White Cat in. Lenny finally adopted White Cat – after much persuasion and insistence on White Cat's side. White Cat then became Lenny's most fervent and loyal disciple.

Many years later, and shortly after White Cat left for other realms, I had a vivid "dream." I was in a small, quiet town, with a small white church and nice old, wood houses lining the narrow streets. On my way to visit the church, and as I was walking down the street, I saw a boy on a bicycle go by. I knew that in the "dream" I was trying to find White Cat, that was the reason for the visit to that particular realm. I wanted to see where she was, and how she was doing in her new realm. Perhaps she was a kitten in one of the beautiful meadows nearby.

More importantly, I remember feeling that White Cat was fine and happy, and had started a new life.

The day after White Cat left for other realms, an interesting thing happened. Perhaps it is a small thing, a minor incident, and perhaps even a coincidence. But at the time it felt significant and brought me much joy. I had known White Cat for many years, and parting is not always an easy thing, even if one is clairvoyant. In any case, I was looking for something in my file cabinet, and found an envelope filled with several hundred dollars that I had stashed away years earlier and forgotten about. Since I was a starving musician at that point in my life, it was quite a treasure. And I considered the money a gift from White Cat, an inheritance of sorts, in return for saving her life on Black Road. For even if the money was mine to begin with, if I was not aware that I had it, I could not spend it. A little cat could not leave me money in a written will. But a little cat could, from another realm, help me to find money I already owned....

Muffin

Muffin was still very small and extraordinarily adorable when I lost her. The thin old woman who lived next door and fed the birds, later said that Muffin had followed after the dogs and me on our walk that morning. Muffin never returned.

The tiny kitten had been brought to me when she was very young, only a few weeks old. She arrived in the woven front basket of a friend's bicycle, and the first time I met her she curled up in the palm of my hand. My little tan dog, Dominique, immediately adopted her. They were soon inseparable, and spent most of their day sharing the LL Bean bed I had bought for Dominique one Christmas.

I was very worried about Muffin's disappearance because we lived on a very busy street. The chance that Muffin might be hit and killed by a car, if she wandered out into the road – or picked up by a stranger and then taken home – seemed very real. Muffin was still only two or three months old, not old enough to find her way home if lost.

After a week went by, I resigned myself to the possibility that little Muffin would never come home, for one reason or another.

After Muffin's disappearance, in that first week or two, I often heard small 'meows' nearby. Now I am rarely clairaudient, but at that time in my life it was not too unusual. In clairaudience, the sounds are not heard inwardly, either in the head – or in the heart, as in locutions. They are heard from outside oneself, as though someone were speaking aloud. Often it is very difficult to determine if the sounds are in this realm or coming from another realm. The only difference I have found is that the sounds are usually either much sweeter, more beautiful – or louder and harsher, cruder, than sounds on the earthly plane. Usually one determines where the sound is coming from empirically – i.e. if no one is standing there, then it must be clairaudience. However, when one is dealing with a small kitten – kittens are notorious for hiding in small and out-of-the-way places and uncommon nooks – it is more difficult to determine.

One day as I was walking between the buildings in back of my house on my way to the church, I again heard many small meows. They did not seem to emanate from any one place, but I carefully searched the barren ground nearby and whatever tufts of grass I could find. The meows were not coming from the buildings; they were outside in the open air, and nearby – and finally I could only conclude that they were coming from another realm.

Then I did a very interesting thing. Without forming a plan, or even an intent, I climbed the fire escape to one of the buildings. The rickety metal-rung stairs led me to a small landing and a door, several stories up. From there I somehow found a handhold and footholds, and lifted myself up over the eave and onto the roof. From my perch on the old, slanted roof, I could see almost the entire town, facing west, with the hills in the distance. This is difficult to express verbally, but that physical overview brought with it an inner freedom and overview, somewhat as when I stood next to Christ on Quarry Bridge. I felt as though Muffin was showing me her view and state of being, as Christ had then. Or as though I were at least partially in another realm myself, happy and free and looking down on our earthly existence as from a great distance. I stayed there for quite some time and then climbed back down again. After my experience on the roof, I never mourned little Muffin again. Nor did I hear any further small, high meows.

 *Simon*

My little cat Nell, towards the end of her life, had a single child I named Simon. I loved him much, and when my two dogs and Nell and I took our daily stroll around the block, Simon would follow at the rear. One day, when Simon was perhaps six months old – he disappeared and never returned to us. I missed him so deeply, that even a year later I would sometimes go out into the garden on Buffalo Street and call his name.

I have mentioned in other places in this volume that our grief can block our natural communication with beings in other realms, can block the natural clairvoyance that we all have. Simon was a good example.

Everyone saw Simon after he disappeared – except me. Louise came by one day and said, "Simon's outside, under your neighbor's car." I rushed outside – and couldn't see him. Friends, neighbors, my students – everyone saw him, except me. Two years later a new little student came in one day and asked, "Who's the little black cat with white feet in the garden?" I looked at my little student and said with a sigh, "That's Simon." I didn't even bother to go outside to look.

Princess was Janet and Lenny's little cat. A week or so before Princess "died," I went to visit Janet. It was a beautiful, sunny day and JF, as I often call her, was working in her front garden, weeding and moving some plants around. As I came up, I saw Princess by the front steps leading up to the house. She was watching Janet working in the garden in such a sad and wistful way that for the first time in the seventeen years I had known her – and for a reason I did not completely understand - I went over and patted her and inwardly said, "It will be all right, Princess." We then went indoors and I thought nothing more about it.

A few days later Janet called and left an urgent message. Something was wrong with Princess. She wasn't eating or drinking. When I clairvoyantly asked what was wrong, I "got" that it was a kidney problem – and that Princess was going to leave her earthly life. I was not allowed to interfere, to prevent it.

I called JF and told her to take Princie to the vet, and we all went together. The veterinarian confirmed that it was a kidney problem, and that the cat was very, very sick. But as we looked at the healthy, plump cat on the examination table, with her silken, healthy fur – it seemed impossible that Princess might leave for other realms.

A few days later Janet called with the message that Princess only had a few hours left, would I come over. I was leaving town for the day, but I stopped at Janet's on the way. And as I approached the house I saw Karima, Princess' mother, who had left for other realms the year before. She was a small bundle of radiant Light standing between the front sidewalk and the house. Karima was with another, more human-sized bright, Radiant Being, and there was so much Light surrounding this Being that I could not make out a form, see who it was. I went inside the house and said my goodbyes to this sweet, gentle cat named Princess. As I was leaving I said to Janet, "Don't worry Janet. Karima and a very Bright Being are outside on the front lawn waiting for Princess." At this, Lenny went outside and sat on the front porch. Perhaps to be near Karima, whom he loved so dearly. But he also well knew that when Princess left, she would immediately go to her mother and the Bright Being that was with her.

For the rest of the day I felt as though I were between realms - this one and a Higher one. When I returned to Ithaca, in early evening, a Bright Being met me on the corner and walked home with me. The Being was so radiant, I could not determine who it was. The very air I traveled through and that surrounded me itself seemed alive, radiant and crystalline. I must admit that these sorts of occurrences are not uncommon in my life, and mostly I do not even ask myself who the radiant Being might be or why they have come. But I would have to assume that in this case, the supernatural Visit was in some way related to Princess' journey to other realms.

 ## Franz

Franz, my little black cat, spent his last few days in my living room listening to a very difficult Rachmaninov Prelude and other big, romantic pieces that I was practicing at the time. Saintly Franz, one of the most gentle and uncomplaining beings that I have ever known.

Franz "died" in my arms, and afterwards I was almost inconsolable. I was lying on the couch in the living room and praying to Our Lady, the Madonna, asking her to take care of my little cat Franz, when suddenly a clairvoyant movie began in my head. It was Our Lady, and She was some distance away and walking slowly towards me. As she approached, I saw that She was holding something small in Her arms. When She was only a few feet away from me, I saw that the little something was my little black cat Franz. Instead of cheering me, for some reason this made my loss feel more poignant, and I said: "But I want to hold him." and I became even more desolate than before. With that, the scene immediately changed – and now I saw a little black kitten, only a few weeks old. He or she was with other kittens, in a room with many toys on the floor. I also saw a bit of a couch and some human feet in the scene before my mind. I could only see feet and not entire humans, because the clairvoyant vision cut the scene to that size and shape – and I could not change it, expand it (I can only see what I am allowed to see). I had no idea what this scene before my mind's eye meant.

Some years later we decided to get two kittens, two boy kittens. As we walked into the house, a friend greeted us and took us to their finished basement. And there was the scene in my vision – there was the room, the human feet – and there was the little black cat I had seen, whom we took home with us and named Sergei.

On the way there, I clairvoyantly saw a little white kitten with scattered black patches – who we also brought home and called Igor Alexander.

80

Angela

My beautiful long-haired cat Angela reached the age of seventeen earth years, raised Sergei and Igor Alexander during her final year here on Earth – and then left for other realms.

The kittens stayed with Angela those last few days, lying happily on the bed upstairs with her while I did my various chores and errands. When I was able I joined them, and on one of these visits during her last day with us – I clairvoyantly saw my dogs Dominique and Guinivere[19], whom Angela had loved so deeply. They were hovering above and a bit in front of Angela as she rested in the upstairs bedroom. It appeared as though a transparent sheet of glass or some other substance, separated us from them. Both dogs had their noses pressed against this glass, or the edge of their realm, and were looking directly at Angela - not at me, but at her. Dominique was actually wagging her tail, a thing she rarely did while on earth. This clairvoyant vision persisted well into evening. Dominique and Guinivere were obviously waiting for Angela, and were there to greet and perhaps guide her to wherever she was supposed to go.

This vigil continued throughout the afternoon and evening, and on one of my visits upstairs, I gently put my hand on Angela's soft head and she left the body soon after. Several hours later, I realized that the clairvoyant vision of my two dogs – had disappeared. And it never returned.

Later, I thought what comfort the presence of Dominique and Guinivere must have given Angela that last day. For if I could see them waiting for her – certainly my little clairvoyant cat could.

---

[19] *Dominique and Guinivere had left for other realms many years earlier.*

Angela Brings Us Leonora
and Figaro Comes for Igor Alexander

Those of you who have read my book *The Spiritual Life of Animals and Plants* already know my entire feline family: Franz, Figaro, Alice and Angela. They all lived into their teens, and left for other realms within a few years of each other. Sergei and Igor Alexander arrived just as Angela and Figaro left for other realms, and Alice passed over two years later. The day Alice died, we went to the SPCA and found little Clarissa, who is mostly white with occasional spots of grey, and brought her home. The boys accepted her immediately, and she slept with Sergei in his little bed until she was old enough to be on her own.

The two boys lived a sort of storybook life together, trying to parent Clarissa together for a year or so. One Saturday M. and I went to Agway to buy something for the garden, and we met Leonora. She was in a cage near the front of the store, waiting to be adopted – and we could not resist her beauty. Long-haired and cream-colored with shades of light taupe running delicately through her fur – with huge, almost human blue eyes – Leonora is a Ragdoll breed cat, and very, very beautiful. To adopt her we had to first fill out papers at the SPCA. We lost no time, and I waited outside the building as M. filled out the forms.

Our SPCA is out in the middle of a field, with hills in the distance. As I stood waiting out in the sun and mild breezes, an angel appeared before me. The Bright Being was about my height, and composed only of Light with no visible form. The Bright Being seemed to be bringing me a message, although I could not hear any words – and I suddenly felt surrounded by Angela's presence. Our meeting lasted some minutes and then the Bright Being moved away and disappeared into another realm.

At the SPCA, M. learned that Leonora was two or so years old, and she had been a mother to at least one litter of children. We brought Leonora home, and the boys immediately adopted her. Clarissa declared war. Within a few days, the boys looked more relaxed, and we noticed that they were happily sleeping together again in their plaid bed – something they had not done since Clarissa's arrival. They also began to protect Leonora from Clarissa, standing between the two girls when Clarissa posed a threat. Being a Ragdoll, Leonora is incapable of aggression or retaliation, and therefore made an easy target for our young Clarissa. One day, after a Clarissa-inspired skirmish, Igor slowly walked over to Clarissa, nonchalantly yet purposefully lifted a paw – and swatted her.

We began to realize that the boys considered Leonora a mother figure, even though she was a few years younger than they were, and almost the same age as Clarissa. With great relief, they also handed her the job of raising Clarissa and gave up their efforts at parenting. We think that because of her size and her long hair – they thought she was Angela. And that Angela sent Leonora to us, to take her place and role in the family.

Not too long after the boys turned six, Igor Alexander suddenly became ill and swiftly left for other realms. I speak more about the events in *A Mystic's Journal*: the inner warning I received in advance; little Igor spending his last days with his nose touching the picture of Our Lady and the Divine Child; Sergei and I seeing and feeling his Presence moments after he left for other realms. [20]

---

[20] *A Mystic's Journal Entries:*

Monday, July 10, 2006
Igor spends most of his time lying on the edge of the living room couch, facing a picture of Our Lady & the Infant Christ. His nose is an inch or two away from it. JF came by & just stood there looking at him. "He's deeply devoted to Our Lady and her Divine Son," I said. She said, "So I see." Well: he is. A light rain tonight. Igor to my right, facing Our Lady and Her Son.

Wednesday, July 12, 1 p.m.
Last night, Igor cried out twice & jumped down from the couch to the floor. I put a flannel sheet down next to him, under the upright piano bench - but he stayed where he was, on the oak floor. Then I took a small picture of Christ & scotch taped it to a leg of the piano bench, inwardly asking that Our Lord take care of little Igor. Igor looked at the picture for some seconds, then curled up on the flannel sheet, with his head next to the picture of Christ. I found him there this morning, & he hasn't moved from that position, his head next to Christ's picture.

Friday, July 14, 1 a.m.
Little sweet Igor rested on the couch, with his nose almost touching the painting of Our Lady holding Her Infant Son, for most of the day & then left for other realms around dinnertime. A sad, very sad day.

Two or so weeks ago, I was carrying him into the kitchen and an inner voice or thought said: "What if little Igor was to leave you soon?" And I answered: "I could not bear it." And then I forgot about it. And now I am living it.

Saturday, July 15, 2 p.m.
I was playing with little Sergei, in the kitchen, when his brother left for other realms yesterday. Sergei suddenly stopped playing with the string, and turned his head to look at something I could not see. Soon after, I felt a very loving presence near me. A few moments later, in my mind's eye, or with the eyes of the soul – now I cannot remember which – I saw through my physical body, to a being of radiant Light directly behind me. I assume that it was an angelic being. And then this bright, radiant being entered me. We became one, in a sense. And during that time, my grief entirely disappeared.

What I did not mention in *A Mystic's Journal* is that I was also clair-voyantly told that Figaro would come for Igor Alexander when the time came. I was actually a bit surprised by this information; I had always assumed that Angela would come for him. But the boys had worshiped Figaro when they were little. In their short amount of time together, Sergei and Igor had tried to comfort their big Brother in his last days, in the small childish ways they could think of. As they had with Angela, they stayed close to him, and licked his head and feet as Figaro gradually became too weak to groom himself.

On our last visit to the veterinarian's with Igor Alexander, I went out-side to reflect on the terrible and sad news we had just received. Our healthy and happy boy was seriously ill and had only a few days left on Earth. While I was standing in the parking lot, a Bright being sudden-ly stood before me. This being was smaller than the Bright Being at the SPCA, and I felt Figaro's presence surround me. As with the being of Light I clairvoyantly saw at the SPCA, this being was also composed entirely of Light and had no visible form. This being stayed with me wordlessly for some minutes and then moved off to the right, into a small wooded area – and stood there until we had left for home.

Whether this being was Figaro's own soul, or an angel sent to inform me that Figaro would escort little Igor to other realms, is not impor-tant to me. What I needed to hear at that moment was that little Igor Alexander would be taken care of. Which of course – he was.

Postscript

I could not possibly relate all the experiences and meetings I have had with those I love in other realms. In some ways it is a very constant con-nection, more as though I continually straddle realms, live in two or more realms simultaneously.

When I decided to become a concert pianist, a Bright being often stood to the right of the piano as I practiced – and occasionally still does. Who this being is, I have no idea. Yet in all the uncountable hours alone at the piano, he or she was my only companion. As I rehearse the nights before a concert, at times more beings from other realms fill the empty chairs while I practice than incarnate beings later come to the concert. And often as I write in my notebooks, I am aware of someone standing over my shoulder, either reading what I am writing or whispering thoughts of encouragement and inspiration I cannot consciously hear.

Since the completion of the original manuscript, several friends have gone on to other realms; two of them gave interviews in the following section of this volume. My wonderful Swedish friend, Inger, died of a serious illness some months after our interview. On hearing the sad news, I inwardly asked her where she was, and she replied: "I don't know," and then she laughed her wonderful laugh. This inner or outer clairaudience generally does not continue indefinitely after someone leaves, usually for only a week or two. I do not understand why this clairaudience is temporary, whereas the visual clairvoyance and more telepathic clairaudience continue... All I have are the experiences, not their explanations.

Another person interviewed for this book also left for other realms within a year, my dear friend Cynthia. In her case, I heard nothing, no outer or inner words – but I did meet her in the back gardens of Windgarth.

Cynthia lived next to us at Windgarth, our cottage on Cayuga Lake. The first time I went to Windgarth following her death, I had gone down to the lake to think about my friend and fellow gardener. Suddenly I was surrounded by a great Brightness. This Brightness began to move towards Cynthia's dock, next to ours, through her gardens – and I followed. Slowly I began to discern more than one Bright being creating the initial Brightness I had seen, and I assumed it was Cynthia and several angels with her. As we walked together towards the dock, my sorrow became pure joy and Lightness, and I stayed with them in the back gardens until I saw them walking towards the dock. Instead of following them, I decided to find Cynthia's husband, to tell him what I had just seen and felt. He was out front of their house, near the small front road that quietly wends itself along the lake. As I approached, he said that he had looked into the back gardens and seen me there, but he could swear that he was seeing his wife – and he began to cry. At that moment I heard myself joyfully say, with a big smile: "But, I am Cynthia." And I must admit that I was surprised at my words, and also a bit embarrassed.

It was only many weeks later, and after much reflection, that I realized his beautiful wife was in some way speaking through me, to announce herself to him – to tell him that she was still very much alive and very happy in her realm. This was not mediumship: I was not in a trance, I was fully conscious – and I knew who I was and where I was in this reality. But perhaps she whispered that sentence, "I am Cynthia," in my ear – or her presence surrounding me was so very strong I wanted her husband to know that she was standing before him, even though he could only perceive my form.

Sometimes I know exactly who is standing before me, but for the most part I do not. This might seem strange, but it really does not matter. The Bright beings are made of the same Brightness, and the negative beings of the same Darkness. I send help and protection to those who need help and protection, healing to those who need healing, speak sternly to the darker beings who are harming others – and welcome and listen carefully to all the Bright beings who are truly holy.

In my understanding, this not knowing is not a lack of clairvoyance. In my readings, a saint was once told by a friend in another realm that all beings must receive permission from God, to either appear to or speak with those still incarnate on Earth.

And if God wanted me to consciously know the identity of all those who stood before me, in other realms – then I would recognize them. However, since I am continually clairvoyant in the sense that I see into other realms while I also perceive this realm – I would be living in a world littered with forms, and would need to learn to see through all these additional forms in my consciousness – what a task that would be! Perhaps this is also one reason why it is said that not to clairvoyantly see the physical form of a being from another realm is a Higher form of Clairvoyance. But to sense their Presence or intuit their forms, to see with the eyes of the soul, is a Higher state of Perception.

I would also like to add that some of the clairvoyant accounts in this volume were experienced in dream state, others in waking state. That some were experienced in dream state does not make them any less clairvoyant or real. In fact, most non-clairvoyants visit other realms while in dream state, and then erroneously dismiss their validity with: "It was only a dream."

No one on Earth will ever be able to explain
all the Mysteries of this universe and the
realms beyond it. That is not the Goal
of our lives on Earth.

Yet, as the years pass, I have grown to feel that my clairvoyance might be of some small use to the world – perhaps an aid to untangle some of the smaller mysteries that intertwine themselves through this physical universe and realms less material.

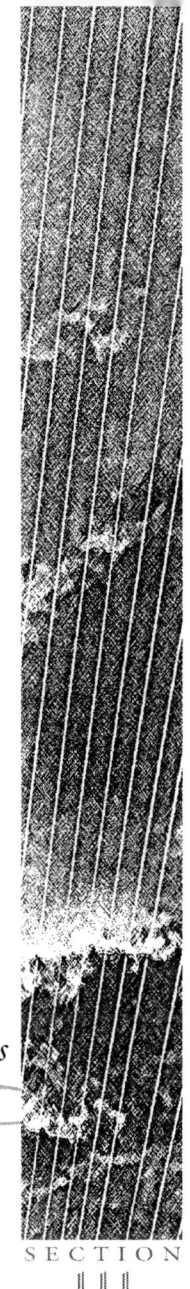

Interviews with Others

SECTION

III

The following interviews cover a wide spectrum and band of human experience: friends I have known for most of my adult life to people I have never met in person; professional clairvoyants to those who had never before had a mystical experience of any sort; housewives, secretaries, a nurse, students, artists, two lawyers, a chef, a policewoman, an eleven-year old and those in university management; interviews by phone, by letter, by e-mail and in person. In writing this volume, I have learned that more people than we suspect have had conscious brushes with mystical or psychic experience.

Some of the experiences related in this section are clairvoyant visions, either outer or inner. Others are vivid "dreams" of meetings in other realms or visits to distant places on this Earth. Some of the people interviewed speak of clairaudient communication, others telepathy. Some experiences are while in waking state, others while in dream state.

Sometimes messages are given from another realm, either personal or prophetic. Other times a "presence" is felt and described, a "feeling" that a loved one is near.

> *These interviews do have at least a few things in*
> *common: they all tell us that our loved ones in*
> *other realms are deeply interested in the lives of*
> *those still on Earth. They also bring messages of*
> *love and peace to those here on Earth.*

After reading these interviews, it would be difficult to believe that our friends and relatives in other realms are as far away as we had thought – or that they have forgotten us, or ceased to love us – as we sometimes fear.

These interviews, in my mind, all also present certain truths. As I mentioned earlier, in Jeremy's story, people to be interviewed for this book often magically appeared seemingly from nowhere. The diversity of people and experiences is astonishing. What most impressed me in these interviews, is that for all their diversity of experience and perception, those interviewed seemed more peaceful and/or wiser as a result of their clairvoyant experience. Even so, I inwardly evaluated each interview very carefully before I included it in this section.

Someone asked me if this book was to help people develop their latent clairvoyance. My answer is: "Definitely not." In my mind, the only safe way to find and perfect clairvoyance is through deep prayer and meditation, or "mental prayer" in St. Teresa of Avila's terminology. Even when developed in this manner there are enough ever-present pitfalls. The clairvoyant has more realms of form to be confused by. More "realities" to decipher and react to. At its highest, the purpose of clairvoyance is to see the Divine Light, the substratum of our universe. The forms – even the most exciting and revelatory – are still forms, images. Therefore, they are not Ultimate Reality or the highest Consciousness. The philosopher/sage Paul Brunton devotes an entire volume of his Notebooks to the dangers of psychic, or lower mystical experience.[21]

When people ask me how to develop their
clairvoyant abilities, I tell them to put them
aside and pray throughout the day instead.
This was how I was taught, and in my opinion,
is the only way to bring the clairvoyance
to its highest level.

Although throughout this book I say in a matter-of-fact or even blasé way that I looked inward to find someone who was in another realm or to go somewhere else on Earth – there is always a sense of awed deep gratitude and great wonder at these times. The inner and outer presence during these experiences is a Beauty and a Clarity that cannot be described. Whether we are contacting our own soul in these true experiences, or the Divine itself – does not really matter. Both are infinitely beyond any other human experience or perception.

The psychic realms and the Mystical realms are literally worlds apart. In true mystical experience, one is surrounded and filled by the Divine Presence. One walks largely unprotected in the psychic realms.

Before I was given training for my clairvoyance and clairsentience, to walk down a busy street or to enter a crowded room could be confusing and sometimes painful. The amount of visual and sensory information given to me was often contradictory and overwhelming. The confusion I felt was compounded by the fact that I thought everyone was clairvoyant and experiencing the same difficulties. At best I felt socially inept, and at worst I became depressed and disoriented. Fortunately, I did receive the proper training. When I met my Teacher, Anthony Damiani – he told me to refuse all such experiences. I also read the

---

[21] *The Sensitives, published by Larson Publications.*

writings of St. Teresa of Avila and other saints of various religions, and culled from those valuable pages whatever instruction I could find.

In my early, more psychic experiences, I was still clairvoyantly accurate. When I suddenly found myself somewhere else on Earth, my friends there saw and heard me. I could accurately describe the room and often what they were saying. When I saw into the future – those events did later happen.

However, for the most part, we have no control over psychic impressions, they come and go as they please. In the psychic world I experienced in my youth, the images were often chaotic and confusing, and many times given to me in symbols. Even if they were shown to me with utmost clarity, my life still remained chaotic and confusing as a result of them. In my experience, even if the psychic experience is a pleasant one, even an enlightening one – our life is disrupted by the experience. The continuity of our waking state consciousness, so important to our psychological balance, is broken by psychic experience. These visions or events are disruptive; they upset our lives instead of enhancing life.

These psychic experiences, even if pleasant or exciting at first, brought a disquiet and discomfort with them – and distanced me from my life on Earth and all that I was to accomplish here. They wrenched me away from ordinary consciousness for longer and longer periods of time, until eventually I could barely tell which realm I was to live in. Nor could I easily relate to the world around me. In fact, the world became more and more painful to me, as well as more confusing.

During and after a true Mystical experience, one is surrounded and infused with Divine Peace and Love, even if the vision itself is horrifying. We are Peaceful and filled with the Higher Love that cannot be expressed or defined in human terms. Often it is a Glow that stays with us for hours, or even days. It does not then turn to a negative emotion or negative thoughts.

One does not feel disquiet or chaos in one's life because of these experiences. If anything, we feel more here, more present, clearer and saner. And we will be perceived as such. Our ability to help others and relate to the world will increase, not shatter.

> *Simply stated, psychic experience entrenches us*
> *still further in the small self, the ego; whereas*
> *true Mystical experience brings us to our own*
> *soul, and ultimately to God.*

After a psychic experience, the psychic's ego responds: "I am great. I just had a special experience. Look at what I did." In psychic experience, if it truthfully be told – the ego is greater and larger than the experience. And we emerge from the experience more egotistical and self-centered than ever, a more willing slave to psychic ways and proclamations. The first proclamation being: "I am better than the rest of the world."

> *In the true mystical experience,*
> *after one has surrendered to the presence of*
> *Higher Love and Peace that accompanies it,*
> *one becomes more humble than before.*
> *Because we have met and seen, known*
> *something far greater than ourselves.*

When I say that I carefully evaluated each interview before including it in this volume, I mean that I have chosen only interviews I consider true experiences. Mystical experiences, given to us by our soul or by the Divine Itself.

Louise Tells her Sister the Future
an Interview with Louise's Sister Jude

Laurie: Have you had any clairvoyant dreams about Louise?

Jude: Both Louise and my ex-husband Mike were in one dream. Mike died in the early 1990's. They were both doing the same work of helping people "cross over" and find their way. I was there with them. We were in a beautiful garden and there was a party there, with people dressed up in long garden party dresses, etc. Louise and Mike approached me at the table. Louise came first, and her body was made of light, not dense in aspect. She was smiling and younger, beautiful, radiant. She brought with her peace and joy, enthusiasm and delight.

Mike came behind her, and he was healthy and robust – and beautiful too, with an aura of peace. He died of muscular dystrophy at the age of forty-one or so. But in the dream he was healthy with vibrant, dynamic energy. He was whole.

Both Louise and Mike were extremely radiant, with a white sparkling luminosity and a gentle smiling beauty – Quietude – Eternal.

I was particularly surprised about Mike, because in this life he wasn't consciously on a spiritual path and not a strong-willed person. In spirit, on the "other side," he explained that he was so limited by the body, and that the body was just a fragment of the real HIM. Now he was able to perform many services for others. There is the Oversoul, or Higher Self, with the smaller egos or parts of us that have extended into matter for a particular experience here on Earth.

They explained to me that they were much more "out of body" than they had been on Earth, and that they could be several places at once, because there was no time frame where they were.

They took me to a corridor, it could have been a bridge – and pointed out wraith-like people who were wandering, lost in the treetops and some reaching out towards us or looking in our direction but not seeing us. Louise and Mike would go to them and guide them into the otherworld. I think these people may have died and been stuck between worlds. Those they were guiding were wanting or seeking to pass over the line between the material and spiritual worlds. The treetops in my dream language are the definitive line between worlds – the material (trees) and spiritual (sky).

Louise is always happy and excited or filled with Awe about how beautiful things are. It's always "Oh Jude, you won't believe how wonderful or how amazing it is here!"

L: *What are your visions like? What do you experience?*

J: In a waking vision I will see symbols, images – or "hear" a voice, or have clairaudient, telepathic hearing. When this is happening, there is an inner knowing. If it is a true experience, you feel it, you know it.[22] In other visions or "journeys," I will go to a special inner haven that I have. Often a white horse or a deer will show up. I have a stone altar there.

In one vision I brought my two children Graham and Olinde with me. At the altar, I asked that we be given healing. A great comforting Light which I equate with the Divine Mother, whatever Her Name (Mary), surrounded us. And as I looked at Graham and Olinde's faces, they shone with a cool white, shimmering light, their faces glowed. The Presence was loving compassion, and had the depth of eternal, transcendent peace, STILLNESS, VASTNESS into which we release our fears, sorrows etc. Sometimes I smell sweet fragrances, like lilacs – and I know a spirit is near.

L: *Have you had waking visions of Louise?*

J: Yes. On "All Soul's Day," I meditated and inwardly asked for any messages my "dead" might have for me and quietly waited. Louise's presence – and this time it was the feeling that she was surrounding me, and also her voice saying "Hi Jude" or "Hey Jude." Of course, tears began to stream down my face. I tell her without words how much I miss her, and that I am mad that she is gone!

The next thing I know, I am in a lake or pool with her, swimming. It is foggy, and the water is warm and soothing. Louise embraces me and tells me: "But I am always here in your heart. And you can come here, to this sacred pool, and swim with me whenever you want."[23] She then tells me that Carolyn, her daughter, will be pregnant in the fall and will give birth to a baby boy. Which you know actually happened! When I told Carolyn the news she said "No way." Then she got pregnant in October.

---

22 *St. Teresa of Avila said the same. In order to weed out false, occult experiences, she categorically dismissed all visions. But she also said that if they had been a true experience, a Mystical one – she intuitively "knew" it.*

23 *This message could be interpreted to mean: "You can meet me in the spiritual Heart at any time." It is there – or in the forehead, the "third eye" as it is termed in the East – that the true clairvoyants receive their "information" and their visions.*

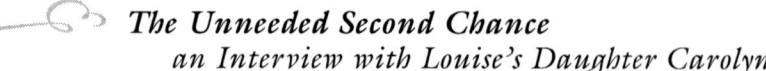

The Unneeded Second Chance
an Interview with Louise's Daughter Carolyn

Laurie: Have you seen your mom, visually, clairvoyantly?

Carolyn: I've seen her in dreams.

In the first dream, I was grieving. I was a little girl – not physically a little girl, but I felt like a child and I was cuddly and grieving. We were in a house in Ithaca, it looked like a meditation room – there were cushions and a futon bed on the floor. My mom and I were both lying down on the bed, she was propped up on cushions. I can tell you exactly what she was wearing: she had on stretch pants, a bright pink sweater and a colorful scarf around her neck – old cowboy boots were nearby, on the floor. She was blonder, and her hair was held back with two barrettes. She looked like she did when we lived in Ithaca, when I was a child. She was wearing her old glasses. She took them off when she was listening to me, and she didn't put them back on. I was so sad. She was holding me, and I was telling her how much I loved her. I said: "You don't understand how much I love you." She said, "I know sweetie." My mom was happy and peaceful, she was great – everything was fine FOR HER. I broke down. She was so tender. She was telling me that it was okay. I was crying and my hair kept falling in my face – she was pushing my hair back from my face, like you do with a small child. She said things to me, but I don't remember what they were. The image that I have – was that she was there to comfort me. After she died, I needed my mom to get me through – but she was the one who had died.

In the dream I got the opportunity to tell her that I missed her and I loved her – and she said "I know, it's okay" – not in words, I'm not sure if she was using words. But the feeling I came away with was that whatever I was feeling – it was fine to have those feelings.

She never apologized, she never said, "I'm so sorry this happened." Or: "Sorry I left, life is cruel. Sorry I can't explain." There was none of that. There was more of the sense of: "You have to know it's all okay." I think she was saying that she wanted us to be together and love each other. And accept things as they were after she left.

And I woke from that dream and I felt that everything was okay. The dream really helped me. This was the first time I felt she had come to me, to help me with my grief. I felt as though I had finally seen her, talked to her.

L: The dream showed you that she loved you, that everything was fine?

C. Yes. In another dream we were at 328 South Cayuga Street in Ithaca, my childhood home. And she was there and I thought since she was there – because in the dream I knew she had died – I thought she had a second chance to live. I decided that I was going to find a treatment for her cancer this time, and make sure she took everything she was supposed to and did the right chemo treatment. So, in the dream I was running around , talking to everybody I could talk to about making sure that this time she would recover.

She wanted to communicate with me, but I was ranting about all that she needed to do and she kept walking away. Whenever I'd go over to her to talk to her about it, she'd walk away or not listen to what I was saying. I remember something about going to the gorge, that part is hazy. I was feeling tortured throughout the whole dream, and at the end – I was emphatically trying to explain to her what she needed to do – and she gave me this look like : "Get a grip on yourself" – and she got in the car and drove away. I ran after the car. I think someone else was in the car with her – I think it was Bert, who had also passed on. I knew she was saying to me: "There's nothing you could have done."

L: Well I agree with that. There was nothing you could have done.

> *It sounds to me that your mom was saying*
> *she didn't need another chance at life –*
> *she is fine where she is and quite alive.*
> *And she just wanted to visit with you.*

C: That's how it was in the dream. I was trying to get her better, and she was trying to be with me.

L: Did this dream feel very real to you? Why did you think it was a real meeting and not just an ordinary dream?

C: Because my mom seemed new and different. I had never had dreams like this with her. Also, I totally had the feeling that she had already been through her life on Earth – and that this was a continuation of her life.

L: In another realm.

C: Yes.

L: It does sound like Louise. To drive off when you wouldn't listen to her.

C: Right. That's the kind of thing she would do. Like: "This is a waste of my energy." She wouldn't participate in anything superfluous when she was on Earth. She wanted only meaningful things and events in her life.

L: I could also see you running around and talking to her doctors, trying to get her healed. Didn't you talk to the doctors when she was so ill with cancer?

C: Well, yes. I talked to her doctors. But I tried to go along with her, I pushed my feelings aside. Her will was not to seek treatment. Instead of speaking up, I would listen to her. I didn't act, but I wanted to. In the dream I was doing all the things I would have done while she was still alive, if she had let me. In the dream, I was fixated on giving her a second chance at life.

L: I wonder what she wanted to say to you.

C: I think she was trying to say, "I'm fine, let it go. Let's do something nice today." She probably wanted to give me a massage or take me to the gorge – the things she wanted to do with me when she was on Earth. And I was fixated on trying to heal her of her cancer.

L: How did your mom look in this dream?

C: She looked the same – except not how she looked in the hospital before she left from her cancer.

L: What was different?

C: In the dreams, she was younger than her real age. She was thinner and totally healthy. Like she was in my childhood. Her hair was a certain way, her clothes were a certain way. She was wearing her old glasses and she had a certain energy – she was the artist in these dreams. If there was an essence to her, then I would say that in the dreams she was her authentic self – the true Louise. She looked like a goddess.

L: That is a beautiful image. Any other recent experiences with your mom?

C: One day recently my little boy, Ian – he's six months old now – was sitting on the couch. I had him sitting up on the couch, and we made eye contact – and I saw my mother in his eyes. It was like his eyes were glass, like a window, and through them I could see the look of my mom, the way she would look at me. And then I started to smile and cry at the same time and I said: "You see me, don't you, Mom?" And I knew that it was her way of saying: "I am here. I see the baby, I see you being a mother." And then I could almost smell her, and I felt her all around, as though she were a halo or cloud around the baby and me. And then she told me that my dad was there too. That they were together, and that they could see me and my family, my children, their grandchildren.

L: I would call your experience an example of clairvoyant superimposition. When this happens, we briefly see the person from the other realm superimposed on someone here on Earth.

In the book I am writing, I mention how it took us so long to feel your mom's presence – that we were blocking the love with our grief. Do you remember how you finally broke through it?

C: It was at a cemetery near my college. I used to go there to eat my lunch. I used to talk to my mom there, and I would ask where she was: "Where are you, I can't feel you." And I would ask her why the world felt so different all of a sudden, since she left. And even though I was a grown woman with a child of my own, I felt like such a little girl. And then one day, it was like I fell into a meditative state. I became aware, almost super-aware, of the rustling of the leaves in the wind and the birds and the smell of the grass. It was as if through all these things, I could feel my mother talking to me, that she was there. And I felt her, I knew that she was saying that everything would be ok, and that she was passing the torch to me, that I was now the mother of my own daughter, and no longer a little girl looking for her mother.

L: What did you mean when you said, "I felt her?"

C: I felt her all around me. It's like a memory, but it's happening in the present. It's stronger, it's so much more real than memory. It's so hard to put this into words. It's like you remember how you felt when they were there with you, when they were in the same room or near you.

L: It is hard to find the words. I'm not sure we have the words. Have you had other dreams about your mom that might have been true meetings?

C: Yes. In this dream my entire family, I think you were there,[24] and a few of my mom's close friends were all at the farm in Pennsylvania. We were having a reunion. The reason we were all gathered there was because of my mom's illness. And we were all waiting for something. I was aware that someone was outside the house and would come in at some point. So I kept looking out the windows, and wherever I looked I saw a gaunt, tired-looking boy of about seventeen. And he was wearing a sort of white toga wrapped around him. He had brown hair and his eyes were sunken in. I knew that he was Death, and if he came inside the house my mom would die. And that was the end of the dream.

Then, at the hospital, four days before my mother died....

L: Was this still the dream?

C: No. This was at the hospital, about four days before my mother died. I was awake. My aunt and I were walking down the hall of the hospital and the boy I had seen in the dream walked by us. But he was dressed normally. He had the same exhausted, blank face. I grabbed my Aunt Beth's arm and said: "O my God, he was in my dream, I saw him." And I told her that he was Death in my dream.

---

[24] *I was there. In my "dream," which I had during this time period, Louise's sister Jude had come to pick me up, to take me to the family farm in Pennsylvania. My friend JF had driven me to a gas station just off a highway, to meet Jude partway. Jude was driving a big, old station wagon, and there were other people in the car. As Jude put my things in the car, I saw a picnic basket in the back of the station wagon, and some blankets. I asked JF if she wanted to come with us, but she declined. I remember telling Jude that it would be my first long car ride since my accident – and I wasn't sure that I was ready. I bravely went anyway. In waking state reality I had not as yet taken a long car ride since my accident, I was still too injured to travel. This was a shared dream with Carolyn. When realities line up in this way in dreams, it is often an indication that the "dream" may be an actual other-realm experience. For instance, if it were an ordinary dream, I might have been uninjured and driven myself to the McConnell farm. The "dream" was so vivid and real that I can still remember small details; for instance, the smell of the gasoline, the messy pile of invoices on the small wooden desk in the garage, and papers that were tacked up on the small bulletin board above it. If I ever walked into that gas station in waking state reality, I would immediately recognize it.*

I had a conversation with Elisabeth today on the phone, and we had an interview. Elisabeth is Carolyn's daughter and Louise's grandchild. She is now eleven years old.

Elisabeth is very blond, like the rest of the McConnell family. The first time I met Elisabeth, she was three years old, and I could still barely even sit up from my car accident. Carolyn had told her that I had hurt my head very badly in an accident. Elisabeth came into the room, sat in my lap and tenderly kissed my head. Chubby, and with big blue eyes, she looked and acted like an angel. She had a wonderful singing voice even then, the same quality of sound and pitch sense as her mother and grandmother. And she knew the words to a seemingly endless string of children's songs. One hot summer's day, when she was five or six years old, Elisabeth and I went to the nearby falls, down past the smaller falls and then a bit through the woods to the stream. The stream has many big and small angular rocks to navigate and the current is swift, so Elisabeth stayed on the shore as I waded out into the stream. Perhaps bored alone on shore watching me, she began to sing – she imitated the big pop singers of the day, rock stars, musical numbers from "Annie" and other tunes from the radio, all with the usual popular style, phrasing and musical delivery. I was already laughing when she launched into Figaro's aria from Mozart's opera – full voice, her beautiful voice echoing off the cliffs – with perfect diction and intonation – and also enough joyful and humorous musical and theatrical exaggeration that I almost lost my footing on the rocks, I was laughing so hard. At which point she sang the aria even louder; it was so loud that even those at the large falls probably heard her.

Another day we went to see Alice Reid, the artistic director of the Ithaca Ballet, and Alice gave her a gypsy tambourine used by some of the corps dancers in some ballet. Alice has an attic full of old and new costumes that I have dipped into for Halloween in the past. And as Carolyn and I walked down the streets of town talking together, Elisabeth ran ahead playing her tambourine – she said it was the best present she had ever received – I couldn't help but think of all the times I had told Carolyn that we would one day all be gypsies in Europe.

When Elisabeth was still fairly small, maybe four years old, she was not feeling well – and when I awoke she told me, very seriously, that she had gone in the back room and prayed to Mary, so that she would get better quickly. Still fairly asleep, I asked myself what she meant, until I remembered that there was a little night light in the form of Our Lady in the back room. Even now I occasionally think of little Elisabeth standing before the night light, praying so intently while the adults slept.

Laurie: Do you remember the angels and fairies you saw in grandma Weeze's[25] room when you were little?

Elisabeth: No I don't.

L: That's okay. Is she coming to see you at bedtime again?

E: Yes. Sometimes. Or she'll be lying on my bed when I come in.

L: Do you see her or do you just feel her?

E: Usually, I just feel her. I can feel it is her. It's almost like I can see her, but I can't see her. When I was really little, I used to feel angels come into my room and lie next to me in bed and play with my hair.

L: What did they look like?

E: It's weird. I didn't see them with my eyes, but I saw them – but I didn't really physically see them there. It's hard to describe. You see them but you don't see them.

L: I totally understand. I have the same problem trying to describe it.

E: Then, when we moved into this house, I was ten years old, I was in the living room and a picture came into my mind. There was a woman, and she was lying on the floor of the living room. And she had red hair, beautiful red hair. And there were demons dancing all around her.

L: Did they all leave? Are they gone now?

E: Yes.

L: That's good. I'm sorry you had to see that. Were you scared?

E: I wasn't scared. It was just strange. There is something else. It's about the colors over people's heads.[26]

L: Okay.

E: One day I was looking at mom's face and the colour over her head

---

25 *Louise*

26 *auras*

was yellow. And mom looked at me and said that I was blue. And I was wondering – what does blue mean?

L: I'm not sure. Blue is a spiritual colour. They say blue means the person is a Healer, many Healers are blue.

E: What color are you?

L: I can't see myself. Your great aunt Jude once said that I was blue. So we're both blue.

E: Blue is my favorite colour.

L: Can you see your own colour when you look in the mirror?

E: No.

L: Neither can I. I should tell you the joke that my friend Donna told me. It's about two clairvoyants. Two clairvoyants meet on the street. They stop and one says to the other: "You look fine, how am I?" When Donna told me this joke everyone in the room laughed. I didn't get the joke I kept waiting for the punch line, because that's the way it really is. We clairvoyants see others, but not ourselves.

There was a long pause on the other end of the line and then Elisabeth finally said: "O, I get it." She wasn't laughing. I found this telling, because we had been laughing through most of our phone interview. As Elisabeth answered my questions, I would slowly and painstakingly repeat the last thing she had said until it was all written down. She thought this very funny and got me laughing as well.

I guess the clairvoyant joke is not meant for clairvoyants.

There was another pause and then Elisabeth said:

E: My fourth grade teacher was violet. My second grade teacher was blue. And my third grade teacher was aqua.

The Forest
a Second Interview with Elisabeth

This interview with Elisabeth was almost two years later. We were at the Lake house, and Elisabeth was drawing with watercolours on the lawn. As I wrote down her answers she quietly painted a portrait of Louise, which she then gave to me to keep.

Laurie: I hear that you had an interesting dream about your grandmother.

Elisabeth: Well, what happened in my dream was – it started out like a nightmare and I was stuck on a mountain. I was in a car and didn't know how to drive it, and the car was about to go off a cliff. It did go off the cliff and I was so scared. And then all of a sudden I was taken out of the car by all the force and I was flying and someone was holding me. At first I was freaked out, but then I had this feeling of peace and tranquility. I looked up and it was grandma Louise holding me. We landed in a place hard to describe. It looked like an Impressionist painting. It was alive and everything was moving, swishing almost. It looked like a painting of a forest, it was blurry; it looked like one of my grandma's paintings.

It was like a wall of blurred swishness and geometric shapes flying through very fast, very alive.

L: How long ago was this dream?

E: Last year. On the anniversary of her death. I had no idea it was the anniversary of her death.

My grandma was behind the wall of blue and green, and I was looking through it to see her. And she said that where we were was the "in-between" of our two realms and she was trying to say to me that she can't be with me as I want her to be. She was telling me how much she loved me and my mom and how much she misses us.

L: What did she look like?

E: The only way I remember her, my only memory of her. She was smiling at me and wearing a bandanna, her maroon bandanna with paisley. She was talking to me about everything and how she wishes she could be with us. She was also trying to explain that she IS with us, but not completely, not physically here – and that she can't be physically with us. It was really beautiful there. It was really peaceful there, but I was hysterically crying.

L: *Because you missed her?*

E: Yes. All I wanted was for her to hold me, but she couldn't because this wall was between us.

The next morning I was telling my mom about the dream and she told me that it was the anniversary of grandma Louise's death.

L: *Your mom also mentioned something about a hand?*

E: When I was maybe six or seven, my parents were temporarily split up. I missed my dad so much and I loved him and I wished that I could be with him. One night, really late at night, I was at the Farm in the back bedroom and my mom was asleep next to me, and I was thinking about my dad and how I loved it when we were together. I started to pray and I asked God that they get back together. I started crying a little and I was just asking the question over and over in my head. And then all of a sudden I felt very peaceful and light.

L: *What do you mean, "light"?*

E: I felt light, like energy. A pure, graceful, gentle beam of Light. I felt this Light around me, flowing through me and into me.

All of a sudden I literally saw this hand come down from the ceiling and I put my hand up. It was a man's hand and he wrapped his arm around my arm. It was about the size of a grown-up's hand.

L: *Was the hand made of Light?*

E: It looked like a sketch. It was transparent; you could just see the outline of it. And I can't explain it, I just knew, I knew that it was the Hand of God. And then, a couple of months later, my parents got back together.

L: *Thank you for this interview, Elisabeth.*

E: You're welcome.

Jeremy

an Interview with his mother Betty

This interview is with Jeremy's mother Betty, who is not clairvoyant. Nor had she ever had any other experiences of clairvoyance or clairaudience prior to these with her son Jeremy.

Betty: The first thing that came to me was in a dream. My dream was very shortly after he died, maybe a few days. I dreamt that I was watching him go through a new world which was all grey. He was moving through something that looked like revolving doors – the kind you might find in a hotel lobby – and he was moving at an incredible speed. And it was just so much like him – that I felt I was actually witnessing him.

Laurie: How do you know this wasn't just an ordinary dream?

B: First of all, I frequently do not remember my dreams. This "dream," I can recall it now as though it was something that actually happened. It seemed very, very real, there was something very solid about it. I can remember the revolving doors as though I were walking through that door. And I can recall it any time, in my mind.

The next thing that happened was at his memorial service. I came early so that I could spend time with him. I was very quiet and was trying to get in contact with him. This is NOT something I usually do. I was hoping to communicate with him, which I did. And I asked him the proverbial question that a parent would ask – I said: "Are you okay, Jeremy?" and he said, "I'm fine mom." I really felt that he answered me. I didn't speak in words, vocally. Then he spoke to me – I felt he spoke in the same way, non-vocally – I suppose it could be called telepathy? It was silent communication.

And after that I somehow felt good through the rest of the ceremony. When you think of the situation, what state I could have been in... I was able to talk to people and I was calm. I would almost say that I felt happy.

And that night when I mentioned it to my son Tony, who doesn't believe in anything like that, he said: "Jeremy helped us all through that ceremony."

A year before the accident my husband got in a panic thinking Jeremy was going to die. Jeremy himself said throughout the years that he was

103

going to die young. He'd say "I'm going to be a pancake on the ground," and he'd laugh about it.

For a month before he died, when I looked across the table at him at meals, I found myself absorbing every physical part of him, as though I was retaining it, putting it inside myself. It was an unsettling thing, what I was doing, I was so intense about it. I would try to look away, at my husband or my other sons Justin and Joel – but my eyes would always go back to Jeremy.

Five days before he died – I hadn't taken pictures of him in years – I had an urge to take pictures of him. Jeremy kept covering his face – the boys did not want me to take pictures of them – but I persisted. Thank goodness, because they are the only pictures I have of Jeremy as an adult.[27]

Then, after the memorial service, there were three things, maybe more that I'm thinking of. There was a lot of emotional torture, where he should be buried; it was a difficult decision. I was meditating one day and I wanted to know what to do with his body.

And what he said was – and again, he "said" it not in words that some-one else could hear – I more felt the words – he said: "It doesn't mat-ter what you do with my body. Just keep the family together." Because the issue was causing a lot of friction in the family.

L: Did he ever actually appear to you?

B: Probably a week or less after he died, I was sitting in the living room, in "my" chair, there's a big chair there that I always sit in – and my hus-band Bob was meditating; he had his back to me, and my son Joli was lying on the couch. Bob was upset with me because I had to cry; I couldn't hold in what I was feeling. Anyway, at the end of that conver-sation, Jeremy entered the room. There were no lights on, the room was very dark. I was not asleep, I was wide awake.

Jeremy was dressed in his blue striped shirt and his black jeans. He was in his own clothes, but he was much bigger than he was in life – he was wider and taller, not fat – he had a huge presence. He was not stand-ing on the floor, he was in the air. This was not something I was imag-ining.

---

[27] *When I looked at these last photographs of Jeremy – I clairvoyantly saw that he had already, in many ways, left for other realms. He was no longer com-pletely in the body. A new Light was already beginning to shine through his body, replacing and draining the physical body of its strength and solidity – in order to make the transition easier. It is difficult to find words for this, but I have seen it in others as well.*

He took his arms and put his arms around the three of us. He was so big that he could reach all of us and embrace us. We were all in different parts of the room. He told me again to keep the family together. I didn't hear a voice, it was more like our conversation at the memorial service.

He was in the room for at least twenty minutes. I felt it was so wonderful that he would stay with us all that time. I felt so connected to him. I was amazed that he stayed so long, and I wanted to see if he would come with me into the kitchen. So I got up – Bob and Joel by this time were both sleeping – and I walked into the kitchen and he came with me. There were lights on in the kitchen and I could still see him.

The presence of love was immense. Throughout this event I felt that he was taking care of us.

He didn't stay in the kitchen for long. Just for a few minutes and then he left, he just vanished. I just couldn't believe it, that he stayed so long and followed me into the kitchen.

He came on his birthday too – that was the latest one. We have him buried in his urn on this little hill above the pond. On the day of his birthday I knew I was going to have a hard time emotionally, so I invited other family members to the house and we had a barbeque outside, which we had also done two years ago for Jeremy's birthday.

We were very happy that day. After we finished the cooking and the eating, which took a few hours, we walked up to the site where he is buried with candles. And we set them beside the stone on the top of the little hill. And I was sitting beside the stone, and my hands were clasped, and all of a sudden – it's as though an energy came into my hands. It was like they came alive, I don't know. It was otherworldly. I had never experienced anything like that. It was like an enormous energy, of love and peace, it was as though instead of embracing me it was just my hands. I've been having so much trouble finding the energy to do anything, the spark feels extinguished – and I felt that Jeremy was giving me energy so that I could go on with my life. It wasn't a visual thing at all. It was as though my hands were moving internally – maybe as though he were holding my hands."

And then Betty looked at me and laughed, her eyes filled with both fathomless sorrow and laughter. She continued: The frustrating thing is that I've had all these experiences, I've been given so much – but they don't last. I'm greedy, I want more. I read a book about a man who channels children for their parents.[28] Some of the children say they are visiting their parents in their dreams, when they are asleep. And almost all of the children say "Thanks for praying for me. Please keep doing it." One said: "I like it when you pray with the beads, it makes me feel good." They meant rosary beads. One child told his parents who weren't very spiritual to say their own prayers, ones they made up.

And I was reading about Jewish mysticism, The Kabbalah – and they say that the only way you can free or redeem the dead, is to pray for them, they are totally dependent on their living loved ones to pray for them.

This is totally foreign to me. I never prayed for anything. But I've started praying for Jeremy – and myself, because I've been so desperate. And when I do it, I feel as though Jeremy is there – so I really want to do it all the time.

L: Non-clairvoyant people are always asking me how to look for "signs" from their loved ones. Did you have any other experiences?

B: Actually, when the spring first started, which is in March, April – I guess I hadn't realized that my life is entirely changed now. So I would go back to things that I had done before, thinking that I was supposed to do them. And I was in the garden, by the gate, and I think I was planting carrots – and it was a windy day, but not very windy. And a plastic bag flew up and stayed directly over my head – for a good minute. And then it flew away.

And it felt just like Jeremy. There was an energy force around the whole scene, and when this sort of thing happens, when there is this enlarged space, or a halo, an energy force around something – Jeremy's personality is there and our entire relationship is there. There was a feeling about it that brought me back to his spirit and our relationship. I feel it as an energy, it fills the air. I can't describe it any better than that.

And this scene with the plastic bag also reminded me very much of Jeremy because he used to like jokes, and to tease me. It was like he was laughing, having fun with me, playing. When he was here, he used to collect the grass clippings that he'd cut and bring them to me in the garden – because I was using it for mulch – and he would throw a huge bagful at me, laughing. And I would be laughing too, like in a snowball fight.

Every time he's come he's happy and playful – he's full of love and caring. He was so frantic and tired the last few years, and would get angry so easily – it was rare that we got a smile. I can honestly say that since he's died I've had many more experiences with him which are wonder-

28 *Our Children Forever – George Anderson's Messages From Children on the Other Side* by *Joel Martin and Patricia Romanowski, Berkley Books.*

ful, in which I find the essence of who he is – what I would always look for when he was here and couldn't find. He was so grumpy, so tired.

When I think about all the experiences I've had, when I start tallying them up – how can you say it's positive when you are feeling so much pain – but the experiences are always happy and wonderful. And my husband Bob has said that too, that Jeremy is always in a good place. One day we both felt him around. Bob asked Justin if he felt anything, but Justin said, "No."

I cannot say that I would choose this, that I wouldn't want him back in a second. Not at this point.

L: Has anything like this happened to you before?

B: My sister has come back in dreams for many years – it's been forty-two years since my sister died. She would come back in dreams, and then it seemed that she was around for about a week. And then nothing would happen for a year or two years. But with my mother and father and grandmother – I never knew my grandfathers on either side – nothing like this happened to me.

I think Jeremy's been so present because he's my child and I am incredibly connected with him. There's so much love between us.

I wonder if the others were or are around, and I just didn't see them.

Inger

One day my wonderful Swedish friend Inger[29] stopped by, and I asked her if I could interview her for this volume. She graciously agreed, and the following is the transcript of our interview.

Laurie: Inger, people often ask me about "lost souls" and what we should do to help them. Have you ever had any experiences with these poor souls?

Inger: Yes, I have. I was once asked to pray for Hitler – I saw his spirit twirling around in nothingness; it looked like outer space. Imagine the pain of that, being alone in nothingness. I was asked to pray for him, so I did.

L: By whom?

I: By my "guide" Elena, who's been with me all my life.

L: Who is she, is she from another realm?

I: No, she was incarnated as a human and now she is a spirit. She took good care of me when I was a child. I never had accidents – I was always curious, always looking into closets, my mother's pills or something like that. I was like a little wind when I was a child. It was like having a mother with me all the time, because I was alone so much of the time. I lost connection with her in my teenage years. When my husband Bernie died, she came back. I always felt someone looking after me.

L: Did you ever see her? What does she look like?

I: She has light hair and very large brown eyes. To me, I am never a good judge of age, she looks in her thirties, a large woman – not fat, but large. She's really laughing at me now.

L: What other experiences have you had?

---

29 *My friend Inger "died" about six months after we had this interview. It was the last time I saw her. When I first heard the news, I inwardly looked for her and found her. I asked: "Where are you?," and she laughed her musical laugh and answered, "I don't know." I said, "It's okay, you'll find out," and we both laughed. At times, her loving presence fills the entire downstairs of my house.*

I: I have some very distinct memories from "astral travel," when I was asleep. One was being in Europe, in a large city, and stopping a child from falling in front of a car.

L: How?

I: I felt like I had a physical body, and I just put myself in front of him, so that he couldn't fall. I can still see what the little boy was wearing – which gave me the clue to where he was. He was wearing little dark blue woolen shorts and grey knee socks – it was in England, it was his school uniform. It feels as though this happened last night, although it was many years ago. I can describe the street. It was a corner, but a rounded corner, and the street was cobbled with stones. And behind him was a building of tan stucco. It was in a big city and it was a very busy corner. I remember the sense of relief and joy afterwards. I woke up and said, "Thank you God." He wasn't supposed to leave yet.

L: So we help others while in dream state, whether we are conscious of it or not?

I: Yes.

In another "dream"... I call them conscious astral experiences – I am asleep, and it is very, very vivid, you feel as though you are really, really there. In this one I just took off and found myself zooming over oceans, until I reached the Himalayas, in what I believe was Tibet. A woman was begging on the street, and she was very, very sad and ashamed. I had to stand there awhile before she looked up. She finally looked up, and I communicated with her through my eyes.

L: Do you think others can see us when we travel in this way?

I: I think that some people can see us. And what I told her is that God loved her. Because she had lost hope. She lit up then, and I left.

I also went to see my husband Bernie after he died. He died in a car accident in 1974. My dream was that a mutual friend – he was a very spiritual man – took me by the hand to a very beautiful valley. He took me to a very large room with only a roof, no walls, and it was very long and rectangular in shape. And inside was a very wide reading stand, it was the length of the room and very large. There were many, many big books there, ancient books, and people were there studying the Word of God. And that's where Bernie was.

Bernie came outside and reached out his hand to me, and our fingertips touched. I was just filled with his Love. I woke up a different person.

L: *How did you know this wasn't just an ordinary, psychological dream?*

I: Because the dream was in full technicolor. And I was so amazed, because later I read books describing where some spirits spend time after leaving the body, and it was exactly like my dream. Also, I can remember every detail clearly, as though it were yesterday, as though I dreamt it last night. And this was almost thirty years ago.

L: *What other experiences have you had?*

I: In July of 1990, my mom was diagnosed with cancer and I went to Sweden for two weeks to take care of her. We were very, very close. I cleaned her house from top to bottom and cooked her a freezer full of food and stocked her with all the medications and supplements she needed. I was riding around town on an old bicycle, because she didn't have a car.

L: *Where were you?*

I: She lived just north of Stockholm, in a town called Upplands – Vasby.

One night, the following November, in a "dream," I was at a train station and I was trying to buy a ticket to go and get my mother. But I open my wallet, and my money is torn in half. I feel a tap on my right shoulder and I turn around – and there is a being behind me at least eight feet tall, made of bright white Light. And the being says: "You have permission – go." So I start running around on the platforms, and I can't find the right train. I get so frustrated that I just kick myself off the Earth, just as though the Earth is made of rubber. And I come up, way, way over the Earth. I can see the Earth below me, and it looks like a beach ball. Then I see a silver cord, and it isn't taut, it's just winding around, floating in the air. I grab it and bring it back to Earth.

I was awakened by the telephone at six a.m. the following morning. It was my stepsister who had called to say "Inger, you had better get here, your mother almost died last night."

L: *Are you ever clairvoyant, do you see into other realms while in waking state consciousness?*

I: I more "feel" things and sometimes hear things. But I was cleaning my house one day and thinking about my relationship with my sister – we were having some problems – I was just standing there awake and conscious, and suddenly I was holding a big, old book. I could feel and see the book. And it was open to a particular page in the life of my sister. I don't want to tell what it was, but it was very, very helpful in my relationship with her.

The book was like the Bible, the letters were lit up like gold, but they weren't really gold. The paper was like onionskin. The print was large and there were two columns on each page. The cover was like pale leather with gold embossed signs on it – I assume they were letters identifying the book.

L: Was the writing on the cover an index to the book?

I: Yes, because there were so many stories and lifetimes in the book – to tell who was in the book, what lifetime. But I just read that one page. It was a very clear short story, written in full sentences – it read like a book.

L: Say more about your clairaudience, when you hear things from other realms.

I: My mother and stepfather had a really hard life together the last ten years of his life. He was a compulsive gambler. He died very suddenly from a heart attack, and I went right away to visit my mother in Sweden. And while I was there, my stepfather came to me every night while I was asleep and he would yell: "Inger, you've got to get your mother to forgive me," over and over until I woke up. He continued even after I woke up, so I lost four nights of sleep straight. I didn't see him, but I heard his voice as clear as a bell – as though he was in the room. Every morning I would go to my mother and beg her to forgive him. And she would go, "Yeh, yeh, yeh, sure, sure, sure."

This continued every night until I finally got her to sit down with me and talk to me. After four days of this I said to her: "Mom, you have to really think about this and really forgive him." So then we sat down and had a real talk, and she realized that she hadn't really forgiven him.

And that's when it all stopped – and I got some sleep.

Another time was with my son Daniel. Daniel drowned off the coast of Oregon on June 21st, 1988. Through the incredible pain, I continually heard his voice, saying : "I'm here, Mom...." over and over and over again.

111

L: In this clairaudience – do you hear their voices from outside yourself, or inwardly?

I: From outside myself, in the room. It's just like anyone talking, like you and me today.

L: Do you ever detect scents in these experiences, like perfumes?

I: The only time I smell something is when my grandpa comes to visit – I can't see him, but I can smell his cigars.

This isn't in dream state, this is in waking state, just walking around during the day. I smell his cigar and I feel his warmth, I feel him emotionally – but I don't see him.

Actually, my guide Elena smells like the flower, what do we call it – lily of the valley.

The Party
an Interview with Meryl

My friend Meryl and I were having dinner at Friendly's together one night, and I told her that I was writing a book about my experiences in other realms. She began describing a dream about her father, and I asked her if she had a pen. This interview – as many of my most important and creative thoughts, messages to myself, and reminders – was scribbled down initially on the back of a paper place mat.

Meryl: I was at a party in the dream, and that part of the dream I do not really remember. My father was at the very end of the dream, right before I woke up. We were sitting across the table from each other, and he was laughing, laughing, laughing. And he looked at me and said: "Why haven't you called me?" It was just like him to say something like that. When he was alive, I'd call him and he'd say: "So, this is my daughter. When did I talk to you last?" I could never call him often enough.

In the dream when he said, "Why haven't you called me?" inside I was thinking, "But I do, I talk to you every day – every morning I say 'Hello daddy, I love you.'" But my answer to him was: "Because you're dead," and I woke up laughing.

Laurie: *What was your dad's response to that?*

M: He was just laughing. I knew that he would think it was funny. I was laughing because I thought it was so funny that he was asking me this.

L: *I guess you got your sense of humor from him.*

M: Yes, I did.

This dream was lots better than the one I had about my mother after she died. I dreamt that she died in my arms – and I woke up crying and screaming.

L: *That was what I call a psychological dream.*

M: Why?

L: *She didn't really die in your arms, in this reality, did she?*

M: No, she didn't. I wasn't even there.

L: *And in the dream about your mother you felt worse after you woke up, not better.*

M: That's true. Now that I think about it, I'm not sure that I've cried about my father since I dreamt about him. I don't think I have. I think because of all the laughter, because I saw him happy, it reassured me that he was okay.

L: *Did the dream about your dad seem real?*

M: Absolutely. I was sorry I woke up.

L: *Was it more vivid than other dreams, was it in color?*

M: Yes. It was very, very clear - his face, his speech. It was as though we were sitting across from each other. I don't remember if the dream was in color, but it was bright - Light, this kind of Light - like in another realm. He was lit, it was like he was emanating Light - it wasn't an external light.

He was so happy. Joy, happiness, Light. He looked healthy - I don't think he was wearing his glasses. He was younger in the dream. He only wore his glasses when he was older. That's odd. I ... don't think he was wearing his glasses.

L: *Was it usual for him to be happy, when he was on Earth?*

M: No, it wasn't. I loved that dream.

L: *Well, in my mind, this was not an ordinary dream. I think it was an actual meeting. Thank you Meryl.*

The Grandfather
an Interview with Meryl's son Conor

Laurie: Your mom told me that you communicate with beings that are "on the other side"?

Conor: I have mostly communicated with my grandfather and my grandmother.

L: Are you awake or asleep when this happens?

C: I am always awake.

L: Do they look the same as when you knew them on Earth?

C: I always see them as healthy and vital and revived. They are the same age as when they died, but they just feel ALIVE with energy and life. My grandfather loves to play golf, so much of the time he tells me what the weather is like, who he is playing golf with and how much fun he is having. My grandparents do everything together. You see, when they were alive, my grandmother loved my grandfather so much but he didn't treat her how she wanted to be treated. He didn't love her enough or express his love enough. Now he is completely transformed and is peaceful, loving, fun, light and easy to be with, and loves my grandmother completely.

One other story I will share with you. One day my girlfriend and I were with two other friends. We were together in their five-year-old's bedroom. I literally could feel another presence, and began to visualize this bald man with short hair on the sides. I asked my friend if his grandfather looked like that, and he said: "Yes." Then I told him that his grandfather was here in the room with us. My friend John began to cry and told us all about his grandfather and how extraordinary he was. That he worked as a coal miner and used to drive eight hours one way just to have dinner with his wife on weekends. And no matter how big, difficult, or strenuous the work he had to do was, he never ever, ever complained, he just said: "This is the work I have to do, and I am going to do it."

And in that moment I could almost see someone standing behind John, ready to catch him if he fell. And I began to tell John that the reason your grandfather has not fully crossed over yet is because he is here to support you... until the way you relate to life is "all there is in front of me is the work to be done" and have no issue about it. It was one of the most amazing communications I have had with someone who has crossed over.

115

The Willow Tree and the Angel

sent to me by Lee-Ellen Marvin

In Santa Cruz, California, there was a lovely, old weeping willow tree in my backyard. It dominated the yard. Children especially loved it because there were two large tree limbs that stretched out across the yard, just right for climbing and swinging. Someone had attached a strong wire from the higher limb to the lower one, to support the branch from breaking under its own weight. On a very hot summer day, I was weeding a little garden patch on the side of the house, and heard a rustle in the willow tree. My first thought was that some sort of animal or bird was in the tree. I wanted to investigate. I was new to California, and interested in all of the plants and animals there – especially the possum that had taken up residence under the deck. But I heard a clear voice in my head saying, "No. Don't go under the tree." And I answered it, "But, I want to see whatever it is in the tree!" And the voice answered me, "Then walk through the house and watch from the other side, you'll see something." I obeyed without considering where that inner voice was coming from. By passing through the house, I got to the side deck just in time to see the two big limbs peel themselves from the side of the tree and come crashing down into the yard. The noise was tremendous; leaves and wood chips were scattered all over the grass; there was a terrible wound in the tree. Neighbors came running out asking me if I was okay. "I'm fine!" I answered quickly. I began to tremble when I realized that I would have been seriously hurt if I had gone under the tree. It was clear to me that a spiritual entity or guardian angel had saved me. The voice was definitely not my own and we had engaged in a real conversation.

It was the most clear experience of spiritual protection I have ever had. It really is possible to be touched by a spiritual power but when I think about this story today, I shudder to think how I had had a choice to follow or disregard the message.

116

The Glass Is Breaking
an Interview with Mabel

Mabel [30] came in, at a vibrant ninety-one years of age, and propped her-self on my living room couch. In spite of her small, frail physical frame, she exuded her usual power and intelligence. In the early 1970's Mabel, with Kate and my Teacher John Payne, founded the Foundation of Light, a Center of Learning and Divine Healing.[31] I have utmost respect for her gentle and pure Light.

Mabel: I think that there are many different kinds of dreams. First there are regular dreams. Then there are confused dreams in the astral realms, I call these astral embroideries. Then there are prophetic dreams. Then there are dreams where we are participating with someone in this realm or in the beyond realm. And then there are dreams where we are being taught or where we teach.

Laurie: When you say "first there are regular dreams" – by this do you mean ordinary, psychological dreams?

M. Yes. A psychological dream helps us to more fully understand our family, friends and others that touch our lives in significant ways.

L: And ourselves, our own being and personality.

M: A prophetic dream will be simple and powerful, simple and direct, so that there is no mistaking its meaning. This kind of dream is allow-ing us time to adjust to whatever unsettling or dramatic event is to take place. As an example of a prophetic dream: Many years ago, when I was in my twenties, I was alone in my apartment, and my father – he was much older than me, he was fifty-five when I was born – he was in his seventies. I had a dream then, in which I was in a room where it was nothing but blackness, it was very dark, there was no light in the room at all. And then there was an opening in the wall at my right, and a cof-fin floated through, in front of me, and went out the left side of the room. And I knew that my father was in the coffin. And that is all there was to the dream, but it was so vivid that it woke me up. I was in a panic because it was so startling to me – the dream was so powerful. And I tried to rationalize it by thinking: "My father isn't ill, even if he is sev-

---

30 *My dear friend Mabel "died" in November of 2005, less than a year after this interview.*

31 *In Ithaca, New York: e-mail address:* fol@clarityconnect.com
   web address: www.foundation-of-light.org

117

enty-seven years old." The dream made such an impression on me that I decided to go home to be with my family that following weekend. And my father seemed well and as usual, but within ten days of the dream, my father was dead.

L: Did he ever appear to you again?

M: I don't see into other worlds. But for some time after, there were strange noises and strange things happening.

L: Do you think he was trying to get your attention?

M: Perhaps to let us know that he was around, that he was there.

This next story is about my husband Bob. All through one winter he had not felt well, although the doctors couldn't find anything of a serious nature. At Christmas time, we invited members of his family to be here with us, and although we did this every year, it never happened that they all could come. Three of his children and their families lived a good distance from here, namely Maine, Washington D.C. and Illinois, so it was significant that all of them could be here. We had a wonderful gathering and a joyous celebration. They all left immediately the following morning. The next day Bob awakened feeling very ill. And as I came into the bedroom where he was lying down, I saw a fleeting figure at the foot of his bed. A figure was standing at the foot of Bob's bed and looking down at him. It was just for a second, but the thought at once went through my consciousness: "That is the Angel of Death." Well I know the theory of the angel of Death, but I tried to put it out of my mind. I must have succeeded, because it didn't come back into my head until after Bob was gone. He died in mid-January, and it was only later that I remembered having seen the figure at the foot of his bed. There were some happenings after he passed on. For one, electric light bulbs kept burning out, bursting out of their sockets.

Then another thing happened. About a week after Bob's passing, my son Richard came to spend the night with me. Bob had a pair of huge, heavy glass bookends. They were so heavy, you would have to use two hands to pick them up – solid, heavy glass. This was a few days after Bob was gone. Richard was sleeping downstairs on a pullout sofa, in the room where these glass bookends were. The next day Richard told me that he had heard a very loud sound in the night. Then we discovered one bookend that looked like it had exploded from the very center of it. There was a hole in the center and cracks extended out from it. It was rather odd. It was just sitting there, all cracked, with a hole in the center of it. It wasn't as though it had been dropped, and nothing had dropped on it. It was just sitting there in this wrecked condition.

Another strange event occurred about two or three weeks after Bob passed on. I wanted a blank tape cassette to record something on, and I didn't have any new ones, and I said to myself: "I must be able to find a used one around here someplace, a tape with something not too important on it." It so happened that Bob convened a class where outside speakers came in, at Cornell. It was an accredited course at Cornell, and he invited interesting speakers to lecture in the course. And he tape-recorded all the classes. He said to me at one time: "You know, some of these are not worth saving." We had boxes and boxes of these from throughout the years he taught. And anyway, I thought as I needed a tape, perhaps I could find one that didn't seem significant enough to keep. So I decided to listen to one, so I could make a judgement on whether it was one to keep, or one to use. I chose at random, but I became interested in what the speaker was saying. Partway through the tape, the speaker's voice trailed off – although you could still hear it in the background faintly. But superimposed on that was Bob's voice very loud and clear saying: "Hello, hello, hello, hello." Isn't that something?

L: So out of all these tapes....

M: Why this tape, out of all the tapes available, did I pick that one out – I had leafed through a whole box of tapes, and chosen this one seemingly at random. Isn't that amazing?

L: So this occurrence might have been a little better than the light bulbs, a little more direct?

M: Let me tell you, I was really startled, and I kept the tape.

L: The events you just described were in waking state consciousness. You also mentioned one prophetic dream. Have you had any dreams that you feel might have been actual meetings with those in other worlds?

M: When my younger brother died, he was only about thirty-nine years old. But he had been ill for quite a while. He was told that he had the circulatory system of a man of seventy, he had not been well for a long time.

The night after his funeral service, I had a dream. He and my older brother were together in the dream, there was no conversation, but I felt a great sense of love between the three of us and we were surrounded by Light. And my brother who had passed on looked young and vigorous and happy. It was a simple dream, very short, nothing else was going on – we were just together with a lot of love and joy. It was just a vignette, no one said anything. But to me, it was a confirmation that

119

age and the effects of illness leave when the physical form dies, when we are in the other dimension. That which survives, the soul, takes on the appearance of the physical body when it was at the height of its well-being.

L: Why do you think this was an actual meeting, and not just an ordinary dream?

M: Because of the impact it made on me. There was a powerfulness about it. And the fact that it happened so close to his parting. Because the nature of the dream was such that it was sending a message to me that all was well.

L: Not the usual chatter.

M: No.

L: Did this dream seem more vivid than usual dreams?

M: Yes it did.

L: Could you describe his body?

M: I was aware of a brilliance, of a Light emanating through the whole situation, the whole dream. I remember the brilliance of it. I feel that it was a real experience. It felt very real.

The Helper
from Diana

My adored mother Patsy was so tender-hearted that when she would see a sad story on the evening news, especially about children being harmed or hurt in some way, she would cry. And when she would tell you about it later, she would cry again.

Even people who barely knew her, loved her.... for good reason: she had a sweet, sincere way of making everyone feel loved and cared for. To my surprise, for several years after she died, peripheral acquaintances like the Federal Express delivery man or the meter reader who didn't even work on that route anymore, would stop by to see her. Her affection was delicious, and so was her cooking, which was one of the ways she made people feel good. At Christmas, she would make forty or fifty batches of peanut brittle – she had an especially delicate recipe that never hurt your teeth like ordinary peanut brittle does – for a wide range of casual connections as well as her big family. She would take it to the pharmacist, the lady at the post office and to literally all the people inside the radius of her daily life, mailing it off in batches to friends out of town, as well.

When she was transitioning, leaving the body (she had cancer) those last few days, she was not quite in this world and not quite in the next. As her consciousness was fading along with her body, she talked without actually talking "to" anyone in the room. Every now and then, fragments of description were coming through. With awe, she was describing being present at accident scenes, like automobile accidents where an entire family was involved. And from what she said, I realized that she was there to help somehow, just through her presence – sort of an angelic assistant, I suppose. She would describe the people and the scene, and I could feel the concern in her tone of voice. But mostly I could feel the healing strength of her compassion.

It was a consoling realization, as she was on her way to other realms, to know that her beautiful soul could still express the loving service, in an ever-wider radius, that had been one of her highest virtues in this life.

121

 *A Conversation with Rick*

Interview 1 with MG

*This interview is about a mutual friend named Rick, who "died" trag-
ically in a boating accident while still a young man. He was a good man
and a good friend, and he spent many a Thanksgiving and Christmas
holiday with us. He had a gentle, quiet presence and a wonderful sense
of humor – and I loved him very much. I knew him mainly through my
work at the television studio, and MG knew him mainly through her
professional work in town.*

*After he "died," I did not dream of him as MG did, nor did he visually
appear to me. But in those first few weeks after he left for other realms,
I periodically, in waking state, looked within and found him in the spiritual Heart. Most often I saw him comfortably sprawled in an old armchair, in his usual relaxed manner. He was glowing with Light and
health and looked very content, peaceful.*

Laurie: You had a dream about our friend Rick after he died?

MG: I did. It was within a week after he died. In the dream he said:
"I'm fine. Everything is all right, and please say hello to the others for
me."

L: What did he look like?

MG: He looked exactly the same, as though he had just walked in the
door. But he was smiling and very happy in a quiet sort of way. You
know, he was so shy. After the dream I felt so relieved and happy and
grateful.

L: Why were you so grateful?

MG: Because I had been so cut up and distraught – I found out about
his death in such a horrible way, reading about it in the newspaper first
thing in the morning. I was grateful that he gave me a message, for me
and others. That he took the trouble to do that, because he was so
happy where he was – that he cared enough to give a message. It carried me through that time. I still felt his presence for several days after
that dream.

L: Did you feel that this was a real experience, a real meeting?

MG: Oh yes. One reason I realized that it was not just a dream, was that
usually when I wake up from dreaming about someone who has died I

am really sad, because then I know they are really dead. This time I woke up and was braced for that sadness, that letdown – but it didn't happen. This time when I woke up, I was happy and at peace. And I could still feel his presence.

L: *Did this feeling stay with you?*

MG: Oh yes, for several days. I still have flashes of that peace when I think of him, even now, five years later. Now, when I think of him, I know that he is at peace, that he is happy. I don't have that wrenching sense of tragedy. I remember him as he appeared to me in the dream.

L: *Are there other reasons why you think this meeting was real?*

MG: Yes. Usually when I have a dream, I have difficulty remembering it even the next day. And it quickly fades from my memory. In this case, I remember our conversation, word for word, even all these years later. Also, the dream was very vivid. I remembered it in the same way I would remember a conversation I had with a person the day before. I didn't have to write the dream down. And now, after all these years, I remember the dream better than any other conversations I had with people around the same time. I couldn't even tell you who I spoke to then, or what we said. Also, it doesn't feel like it happened a long time ago; it feels like it happened very recently.

I knew I had spoken to him. In a way, it doesn't feel at all surprising or unusual. I simply had a conversation with my friend Rick.

123

The Grandmother

Laurie: What was your grandmother like?

MG: She was of Scottish parentage, and after my grandfather died she lived alone for another twenty years, with only her housekeeper who had served the family for a total of fifty years. During the last year of her life, she was no longer able to take care of herself, and she was in a retirement community. Living in a former British colony – she was very British, and upheld the British traditions of her ancestors. She "out-Britished the British" we always used to joke.

You could set your watch by her daily routine. She always got up at 8am, took her bath, had breakfast, and the rest of her day was punctuated by teas. Morning tea at 10am, lunch at 1pm, afternoon tea at 4pm, and dinner at 7pm.

Afternoon tea was an elaborate affair. Tea was served in her beautiful china tea set, with five or six different kinds of home-baked biscuits, "cookies," we would say here in America. There were date squares, snickerdoodles – which were basically butter cookies rolled in cinnamon sugar – jam tarts, and wonderful cheese biscuits. And there were home-made mince pies for Christmas. Everything was homemade. Despite the often sweltering heat of Christmas Day, the whole family came down and tucked into a traditional Christmas dinner, including: turkey, ham, roast potatoes, and plum pudding with brandy sauce.

My grandmother lived within walking distance from the university my brother Deon and I attended. Deon is ten years older than I am, so he went there for five years and five years later I started at the same university. Each one of us visited our grandmother regularly during our years as students. A beautiful porcelain jar filled with her homemade meringues stood on the sideboard. She used to say: "I always knew when Deon came to visit while I was out, because the meringue jar would be empty."

When I was at the university, I often went to visit her for afternoon tea. We always sat down to tea at exactly four p.m. There were three clocks in her apartment, a large grandfather clock and two smaller mantle clocks that all chimed on the quarter hour. They were all slightly out of sync. So on the hour it was quite a racket for a few seconds. After tea, she took her daily constitutional and I would walk with her.

She was loving in a reserved way. She was very dignified. She lived through the two World Wars, much turmoil in her own country, and many family tragedies with a strength and serenity that provided an anchor for the entire family.

L: And you felt a deep connection with her after she "died"?

MG: With my grandmother, it wasn't a clear dream, it was more a sense of her presence. She died at the age of 97, and I saw her about a month before she died. Because we lived in different countries, I didn't see her very often. And that was my chance to say goodbye.

When I saw her, she mostly did not seem to understand what was going on around her, or recognize people. But at one point she asked for ice cream, and my mother told her there wasn't any. I told her that I would get her some. She looked right at me and said, with all her usual dignity: "You would? Jolly good show."

After she died, I felt her presence very strongly. I felt that she was, in fact, more real and closer than she had been when she was alive. I talked to her often.

L: What do you mean by "presence?" Could you describe it?

MG: I don't know how to describe it. I just knew she was there. I would see her. But it wasn't the body as it used to be. It would be fleeting, like a glimpse. Everywhere I was, she was beside me. I felt comforted. I felt it as a sense of peace.

L: I don't understand. What do you mean by "fleeting"?

MG: I would be coming down the stairs and I would just catch a glimpse of her. She looked as she had in life, and she seemed very serene. She had a lightness about her; she seemed very happy and free. Or I'd round a corner and catch a glimpse of her just leaving. It wasn't frightening or disconcerting.

It lessened over time. It was very intense at first, right after she died. Over the years it has decreased, but I still occasionally feel her comforting presence.

I really think she came to comfort and reassure me after she died, to tell me that she was fine and that she loved me.

 ## A Visit with Bill

Laurie: You had another experience recently, didn't you?

MG: Yes. I was walking to work as always, early in the morning. It was a beautiful summer's day. I usually say prayers as I walk. My dear friend and colleague Bill had died about three months earlier and since his death I have said a special prayer for him and for his family each morning on the way to work. I started doing this because Bill and I often talked to each other on the phone early in the morning before most other people had started their work day. After he died, I missed our early calls terribly, until I realized that I could still talk to him inwardly. When I do so, I have a very strong sense of his presence. I often ask him for his advice and feedback about work-related matters, as I did from time to time when he was on Earth.

L: And do you hear an answer?

MG: Not in the usual sense. But yes, in that it becomes very clear to me how I should handle the situation. I become very still and then the answer comes to me. And sometimes, when I figure it out, I see Bill smiling at me. Once or twice, when I was on the wrong track, he frowned.

At this time, I was asking our colleagues for donations in Bill's memory for the Relay For Life, a fundraiser for The American Cancer Society. Our colleagues answered with great generosity and warmth.

On this particular morning, I was walking to work, saying my prayers and thinking about the wonderful response from our colleagues. I had not yet reached the point in my prayers when I prayed for Bill and his family. As I was about to cross the bridge over the stream that runs near Bill's office, the sense of his presence was overwhelming and I stopped in my tracks. I found myself saying: "Okay, Bill, I'll switch to the prayers for you and your family now."

L: Did you actually see him?

MG: I saw his face and he looked exactly the way he did when he was on Earth. He was radiantly happy, and maybe his presence there that day was a "thank you" to all his colleagues for expressing their love and admiration for him. I didn't see his body, but I saw his face with a big smile and the usual twinkle in his eye. His presence filled the entire bridge and road.

L: *Visually or as a presence?*

MG: I felt it. The force was strong enough to physically stop me from walking any further – which was remarkable, because I usually walk very fast and not much slows me down.

L: *So it felt like a physical barrier?*

MG: Yes. It was an amazing experience. I was so happy to be standing there with Bill's presence all around me.

L: *How long did this experience last?*

MG: Maybe a few minutes, but his presence lingered with me as I continued walking. It's here now.

L: *Yes it is.*

MG: I said the prayers, chatted with Bill for a few minutes and then continued walking. Now I stop on that bridge each morning on my way to work to say hello to Bill.

L: *Have you seen him there again?*

MG: Never in the same way. Most mornings I feel his presence there, sometimes it's stronger than at other times. It's so hard to talk about this....

L: *You know, at some point you will have to let him go.... You don't want to hold him back from his journey in other realms.*

MG: Yes, I understand that. Knowing that helps me, although it's very hard. I know that he can help so many more people from where he is now. He is so free and powerful where he is now.

 *Samantha*
an Interview with her owner Cindy

Cindy: Samantha means Star Soul. I always called her Sam. She was a little deformed kitty, four or five months old when I got her.

Sam was always there for me. I found out that she had cancer when she was thirteen. I put her in my meditation room, and she would lie on the red shawl that the Shankara[32] had given me in India, the day I left.

I was working at this time. About two days before she died, I asked her to come back to me after she left and tell me that she was okay.

I put her in the room with Shankara's shawl; she was probably there for three weeks. I ran home from work every day, as soon as I could. She kept looking up at my altar – so I brought Ramana's[33] picture down. And she was just glued to it. I moved the picture, and she moved. To test it, I brought down another picture, of Anthony or Paul Brunton or someone else – and she didn't pay any attention to it. She turned and looked at Ramana again. During the whole three week period, that photo of Ramana was her constant companion. Her attention never wavered – in these photos, I was taking pictures of her with a flash camera. A few days after she died, I woke up to her purring. She was there. I went to pat her – and she was gone. She had come to tell me that she was fine.

Laurie: Have you had any other experiences of this nature?

C: After my car accident, I had a dream. In the dream I was coming down the stairs of my home, and I opened the front door – and a woman with coal black hair was just standing there. She scared me. I screamed and slammed the door and woke up. A couple of minutes later I went back into the same dream, and I was in the living room and I looked out the window and she was gone. I decided to look in the back yard, so I went out on my porch to the back door. I wasn't afraid anymore. I saw her, the same woman – in a long white gown and with her arms outstretched, looking upward, her arms embracing the full moon above her. And to her right was a deep hole and it had a sign on it. I went outside and saw that it was a deep grave and the sign said: POSTPONED. Then a man's voice, it was God's Voice I think, said:

---

32 *Shankaracharya of Kanchi (bn. 1894) and Sri Ramana Marharshi (1879-1950) were both Hindu Indian Sages. Cindy visited Shankara in India shortly before his demise, in the early 1990's.*

33 *See previous footnote.*

"You have three more things you must do before you go home."

L: How do you know it wasn't just a psychological dream?

C: For one thing it was very vivid. I never forgot it and I didn't have to write it down. You just know they're different than ordinary dreams.

ADDENDUM

L: In Cindy's "dream," she was not specifically told the three things she had to do on Earth before she would be allowed to leave for other realms. Those three things could be anything: to learn the Higher Love, to correct other personal errors or flaws, to forgive everyone (or a specific person), to attain a certain state in her meditations, or physical actions in the world that could affect the destinies of others, etc. This is similar to the typed pages of WHY I RETURNED TO EARTH that I was shown, but could not read, in the ambulance after my car accident (see the story "A Fax From Another Realm").

 *Ilse & Peter*

The Adventure of the Falling Trays

I have never met Ilse, except by e-mail. She was sent to me by the Distant Healing Network, and these e-mails were sent after her husband Peter left for other realms. Her husband must have led a very pure life, for he was immediately taken to a high realm.

⁓

L: Hello dear Ilse! I am sorry to hear the sad news of your beloved Peter. I saw clairvoyantly from the first that Peter had an appointment in another realm. That is why he was not allowed to stay here longer. The transition was in place many days ago. I tried gently to prepare you.

I will continue to clairvoyantly check up on him. Send him your prayers and your Love. Your relationship is eternal, that Love is forever. I was "told" that you will be together again, and that he has gone ahead to prepare a place for you both. Meanwhile, live your Life with the joy of that knowledge.

If you are sensitive, you will feel his Loving Presence near you. Perhaps you will meet in dreams that are more than dreams, that are actual meetings in other realms while in dream state.

Please continue to keep in touch. – Laurie

⁓

Ilse: Dear Laurie: I can't help but think that Peter is here sometimes. I feel that Peter is trying to reach me, but I don't know how to respond.

My niece and I were with him at the end. This past month he was in terrible pain from the cancer and I was so helpless to help him. I could only give him his morphine, which didn't always help.

P.S. I just heard an awful crash in the living room and I ran in to find that the standard with the TV trays had fallen forward and I cannot think of any reason why they would do that. P.P.S. Do you think our two kitties see him? They sometimes seem like they are looking at something I can't see.

⁓

Laurie: Hello Ilse! Interesting that you mention the cats – animals are often clairvoyant. Well, it certainly does sound as though Peter is trying to contact you – well has contacted you. The way to respond – just talk to him, as though he were still in the body. He will hear you. You might also mention that he doesn't have to knock over trays to get your attention – you will just assume that he is there when you need him. It is much easier to go from realm to realm without our physical bodies!

✌

I: Dear Laurie: Another strange thing..... Whenever Peter would sit in his recliner, my cat Tyger would jump up and take it away from him. Or, if we were out somewhere, when we came home, Tyger would be sleeping in that recliner. Since Peter is no longer here, Tyger will not go near the chair ...... And this was one of his favorite spots to take a nap!

I cannot understand this. There are things that come up missing that I can't explain, and of course there is that episode with the TV trays.

✌

L: *Hello Ilse! It sounds like Peter is probably sitting in the chair. Where he is now, he is experiencing more joy than we could ever imagine. And I know that he wishes to share the Joy with you. Try to be with him where he is now, not where he was while he was suffering.*

Those in other realms wish us to be with them where they are now – not where they were in our last painful memories of them. If we put ourselves in their position, this is easy to understand. The relationship continues, it has not ended just because they left the physical body. And from the realm they are now in, they have an understanding and an overview of themselves and the years remaining to us here on Earth – that we do not and cannot have. Those in higher realms will pray for us and try to help us. They will shower Love on us, if we allow it.

131

 *Maureen and the Bus*

I have never met Maureen in person. This interview was conducted over the phone one mild and rainy night in November 2002.

Laurie: Hello, Maureen. Your sister tells me that you have had some interesting dreams.

Maureen: What would I say, except in dreams, you wake up – or there is a sensation or feeling – and then later it happens.

L: Do you mean that what you dreamt about or felt actually happens later, in your waking life?

M: Yes. It's every now and then. I would dream of someone, troubling dreams. For instance, in the dream I will see an accident, and there will be hurt people around, and I am trying to help a friend. And then I will call my friend who is in Norway still, and I will find that she has difficulty in her life then, in her relationships, something was going on then. What do you call this?

L: So it is more symbolic.

M: It is symbols.

L: And you are dreaming of someone in the present and alive on Earth, not of the future or of someone in another realm. This is a form of clairvoyance. Are you clairvoyant, like your sister Anna?

M: No. But I go to a psychic every now and then. And once he said: "Your mother is standing right next to you." And I could feel that, I knew that. I know that she is always watching over me. I can feel her. I badly want to see something, but I can't. I try to touch her, sometimes I just wave my arms around in the air trying to touch her, find her. I have learned to just talk to her.

L: As though she is there with you – in other words, you are assuming that she is there.

M: Yes.

L: Have you had any dreams about people who are in other realms?

M: A few months before my mother died, I had many dreams. Weird dreams. In one, my mother was getting on the wrong bus and I can't stop her, although I am trying to help her get her off this bus. I see her at the back window of the bus, waving to me, maybe asking for help. Perhaps these dreams were to prepare me, because two months later she died. What do you call these dreams?

L: We sometimes call these prophetic dreams, when we dream of the future.

M: The dream was very, very real. You wake up and you think that it has really happened, that you were there. I still see her in that bus, waving to me very upset in the back window.

L: That is a sad dream. But your clairvoyance is very symbolical, it veils itself in symbols. For instance, the dream you spoke about earlier, when you dreamt that your friend was in an accident. But your friend wasn't in an accident. The dream symbolized her emotional turmoil. If you would, please change the dream about your mother, in your mind. From now on, when you think of the dream, picture your mother happily waving goodbye to you through the back window.

> *The dream seems to be a mixture of clairvoyance*
> *and your own fears. I think you added your own*
> *fears to it — your fear that your mom would want*
> *to stay on Earth, or that she wouldn't know*
> *where to go when she left the body.*
> *Clairvoyantly I get that her transition was*
> *perfectly arranged, and that she went to the*
> *right realm — there were no problems.*
> *And she is very happy.*

M: Thank you, I feel a big weight rolling off me. I think now I will not be bothered by this dream again.

I also had dreams about my father before he died, not as clear as the dream about my mother. It was more an unsettling feeling when I woke up, that I know I need to call him on the telephone. Again, it was two or three months before he died, this dream. I think again it was to prepare me.

L: Yes, I think so too. Have you had any dreams of your parents since they passed on to other realms?

M: No. Not that I remember. But when my little boy was about three years old – we were moving to another city then – I went into his room in the morning and he said that there was a man sitting on his bed. And he described my father perfectly. My son was only three years old, so he had never met my father, never even seen photos of him. My father wore big, thick old-fashioned black rimmed glasses.... And my son said that the man sitting on the bed said that my little boy could take all his toys to our new house in the new city.

L: So the clairvoyance skipped a generation in your case. This is not unusual.

M: I do not see like my sister Anna, but every now and then I will smell something. It is so real, sometimes I speak to my sister about this. And I will look everywhere to see what it is that I smell, but nothing is there. And I will ask my husband if he smells something, and he will say "no."

L: Nothing of this world at least. Thank you so much for this interview, Maureen.

Willie's Song
an Interview with Theresa Kulat

Theresa: Starting in the mid – 1990's, whenever I went to funerals I would spontaneously, and internally compose the most beautiful poetry. Because it was inside and so fast, it was never written down, but the experience was very profound.

When my aunt died in 1997, I remember being in the funeral parlor and being aware of her presence. I could tell when she was in the room.

Several weeks later, I got the sense that she was talking to me. She was an excellent watercolor artist, and I had the sense that she was asking me to tell her granddaughter that when the little girl was painting she should think about how grandma would do it – and that my aunt would help her.

The next incident involved Willie, a friend of my husband, Scott. When I met Scott in 1992, he had known Willie for many years. At that time, Willie was in his late 40's and had never married. He really wanted a wife and a family but things just never worked out. He had a heart of gold but was just so high energy that it was hard to be around him. He played on every sport team that my husband did – volleyball, softball, basketball and would go out playing darts, to baseball games. I would complain that Scott spent more time with Willie than with me. In the fall of 1997 Willie finally gets married. In the spring of 1998, they had a little girl named Kelsey.

In September of 1998 Willie was killed in a car crash. It was in the early morning, on his way to work. He was driving down a long rural highway, and was involved in a head-on collision with a local business man. It was very strange and the police were still trying to figure out what happened.

Either that night or the next day, Willie showed up. I am not clairvoyant – I didn't see him. I am clairaudient – I can hear him. And I am clairsentient – I can feel his presence.

Laurie: When you say that you are clairaudient – do you hear him outwardly, as though he is in the room – or inwardly? There are many forms of clairaudience. Is it a two-way conversation?

Theresa: The dialogue is internal. I hear complete sentences. It is generally just like having a conversation with an incarnated person. And there is always a sense of love from the deceased person. To describe the

135

inner ear – it's like singing a song in your head. Let's use the Beatles song, "Let it Be." It's like hearing the song in your head. Not knowing what it sounds like to you, I can only say that my inner ear is as accurate as my outer ear. I can hear every note, every instrument, every word. If I have forgotten part of the song, I can "play it" in my head.

With Willie, it was definitely a two-way conversation. He sounded like himself – a totally spastic person. He spoke very fast, he used the same type of words.

L: *Are you saying that Willie, when incarnate, spoke very quickly – and when you heard him inwardly, he was speaking in his usual way and using the same sort of words he used while on Earth?*

T: Yes. The "sound" of Willie's voice was the same as it was when he was alive. Only it was audible to the inner ear not the outer. It is too bad you never met him because he had a very unique presence – high energy, a little goofy, lovable with a slight lisp. When he crossed over, he was confused and nervous. So the "voice" was his same voice with that added emotion. And he was anxious because he did not quite want to deal with the truth of his death.

L: *Did Willie say more?*

T: Yes. He goes on and on about how I need to talk to my husband Scott and to his wife. He was so sorry that he died. It was an accident – he is so sorry. He is so sad about their daughter Kelsey. Tell Scott he has to write Kelsey a letter about who her dad was. Scott knew him better than anyone. I told Scott. My husband (even though he is very conservative spiritually) agreed that it would be a good idea and he made a commitment to do that.

I will admit that it was the first time it ever happened so strongly and that I was a little freaked out myself. I decided that I would stay in a loving space and that I was willing to be of service if this was how I was called to serve. Willie was also there at his funeral.

L: *What did you experience?*

T: When I say Willie was at the funeral – and I have felt my aunt at her funeral and another young, eleven year-old girl at hers. I do not see them, I do not hear them. It is a sensory thing. I can "feel" that a center of love is in a particular location.

Willie went to a bar with the group. It was one of the team's regular bars that I did not usually visit. While we were in the bar, I played the juke box. After I put my money in, I looked at the titles and ran my hand down the names. I would intuitively stop once in a while and my hand did a funny thing that was kind of like playing the piano. I chose "Friends in Low Places" by Garth Brooks and two other songs. When "Friends" came on – everyone got quiet and Scott looked at me. He said: "That was Willie's song." I did not know that.

We didn't really tell anyone about the experience. I wasn't sure how people would take it. A week or so later, I decided to talk to his wife (he did say at the beginning that I needed to talk to her). So I called her up and told her about how Willie was so sorry and that it was an accident and he loved her and he was so sorry and he missed her (I am trying to communicate in the same hyperactive way that he was speaking). So she breaks down crying and tells me that she and Willie had a fight that morning. She was thinking that maybe he killed himself because he was so mad at her or that because of their fight somehow she caused his death. It was really moving. I kept speaking for Willie and telling her how much he loved her and how it was an accident and how sorry he was. Enough said – you get the picture.

L: It is a moving story. Have you had other experiences?

T: In October of 2002, I attended a Collaborative Law training in Chicago. My divorce had been finalized about 4 months earlier. At this training, I met a man named Forrest. We engaged in some very esoteric banter at the training. A few days later we spoke on the phone and within a week were – what I called "dating." Not exclusive. Just a very playful, mutual respect in a man-woman sort of way. I had not even flirted with a man in 12 years.

We spoke on the phone or in person every day for eight weeks. Around week four or five, on a weekend that I had my kids, he came over for the day. All four of us went to Target, had lunch, played Legos. Forrest sang. Ben, the 2-year old, made up crazy songs.

So I had a wonderful (and challenging) eight weeks reconnecting with being a woman again. He was great with my kids. I did not fool myself into thinking the relationship was more than it was. He saw my boys a few more times after that.

On Dec. 22 he and I went Christmas caroling. That evening, Scott brought my boys home and they met Forrest. Forrest was part of our family – crazy evening – dinner, baths, bedtime. Then he went home. We were not together on Christmas eve or day though we spoke on the phone. On Friday, Dec. 27 Forrest flew to New York for a vacation. I spoke to him Sunday morning, Dec. 29.

Later that day, I was at the dining room table with my boys, Kevin to my right and Ben to my left. Ben looked to his left (toward our family room) and said, "Who's 'at?" (meaning who is that?) I ignored him. Again, he said, "Who's 'at?" I ignored him again. After the third time, I took a deep breath and addressed Kevin, the older boy (seven years old). "Kevin," I said, "I would like to teach you something. There are some people who do not have bodies. They exist but they aren't like us." "Like angels?" he said. "Yes, you could say that. Well, I have told the spirits that they can come here if they are good and loving. It seems like Ben can see a spirit so we are going to pray for this person. If they are good, they can stay and if not, they will leave." So I walked over to the spot he was addressing, sprayed some flower essences for purification and said a prayer.

I walked back to my spot at the head of the table. A few minutes later, Ben looks up and says, "Who's 'at?" "Well, I guess it is a good spirit who loves us. So it can stay." And we finished our meal.

That night, Scott picked the boys up and they slept at his house. Monday morning, I was getting life in order. I was answering e-mail and forwarding a name to Forrest of a woman who was doing work with children that I thought he might benefit from networking with. The phone rang. It was Forrest's assistant. She told me that he had died the night before. I was shocked. I dealt with my grief in ways that are too personal to go into here. They did not have details of a funeral yet because the body had to be shipped and the close relatives were out of town too. The next day, Dec. 30, I had the boys. Midday meal, Ben looks over to the same spot and says, "Who's 'at guy?"

Well, at this point I knew it was Forrest. I explained that he had died and that he loved them so it was okay that he was there. Later I learned that on Sunday, Dec 29, Forrest had a stroke around 11:00 our time. He must have been out of his body when he visited us the first time. There were a few more times after that that Ben would address him.

L: How many times in all, would you say?

T: Ben saw Forrest on 12/29 (the day Forrest was unconscious), 12/31 – New Year's Eve, and 1/1, the next day. Scott then took the boys back to his house for the week. When Ben got back on the next Sunday, he said Forrest was there again. I would say he saw him every day after that for about a week. I did not hear anything with Forrest.

L: That is not unusual, in my experience. Our grief can block the communication, even if we are fully clairvoyant and clairaudient. Thank you for this interview, Theresa.

The Key
from Linda Ruth

*My friend Linda Ruth stopped by before dinner, and I asked her to tell
me about the events surrounding her recent trip to Florida. She had gone
to be with her father in his last hours. I think this story might be especially helpful to non-clairvoyants. Often the signs we are given from loved
ones in other realms are not terribly spectacular, nor even very out of the
ordinary. And yet if we are alert to them, we can gain much comfort
and even joy from them. Most of the signs my friend Linda speaks about
– except perhaps the incident of the wall plaque – are fairly ordinary.
Yet, from the insight and shared love gained from them, we could think
that even the most simple and humble coincidences in this story – such
as the red, white and blue clothes for her dad – might have been orchestrated from other realms.*

Linda: On Friday, January 23rd – I got home from the "Light in
Winter" music Festival in Ithaca. There was a message from my sister on
my phone machine telling me that my father had taken a very bad fall
outside the grocery store in Florida, and he had been rushed to the hospital. He had a "head bleed" and was in a coma. I knew immediately
that this was the end of his life.

I decided to just wait and stay centered. I slept soundly, and the next
morning woke up experiencing a sense of deep peace. His condition was
the same. I felt calm, and decided that I wanted to spend the day experiencing my connection with my father alone, rather than struggle with
airplane reservations, taxis and noisy traffic. I attended another event of
the music festival focused around the sound of the whale. It took me to
wordless places in my heart, where I felt that I could hold my father's
death in deep awareness. I then spent five hours typing a five-page poem
I had written to him for his 85th birthday just two months earlier. Back
in November, something had compelled me to record my memories of
him from the time I was a child. When I read it to him at his birthday
party, he listened intently, which was unusual because of his dementia.
And then with a smile and typical subtle humor, remarked, "That
sounds like my obituary." Exactly two months later he was gone.

I had promised to e-mail a copy of the poem to my family, but had never
done it. The next day, Sunday morning, I woke up anxious and frantic.
I knew I had to get on a plane and go. I arrived there at one in the
morning, greeted my mom, slept a few hours, then went to the hospital at seven a.m. My three siblings had already arrived. One of my brothers lives in Italy, but he just "happened" to be in South Carolina at the
time, the state just above Florida. At eleven a.m., when hospice was due

to arrive, we were all gathered in the hospital room. My sister had put a little American flag in his hand. There was a gigantic one flying outside his hospital room. (My dad was the supreme patriot. When we were children, he was always teaching us to salute the flag and honor the great nation we were born into.) As it turned out, my father made it clear that hospice was not needed. His breathing gradually got slower and slower and slower – and we suddenly realized that he wasn't breathing anymore. It was so gentle.... no suffering and no fear.

His countenance was glowing, radiant and very young. I was allowed to stay in the hospital room with him for several hours, thanking him, weeping, stroking his arm and placing kisses on his forehead. That too felt like a gift. When you stay, you get the peace, the radiance. Grace descends, the angels come. In my experience, it makes death acceptable, you see how liberating death can be.

As I was leaving the hospital, oddly I didn't feel that I was leaving my father. If you are not pinning the person to their body, then nothing has, in fact, left. In the last few years, my father had suffered from dementia. But over the next few days, I felt that my father was in his true power again – the "captain of the ship" again. I felt that he made all the arrangements, so that everything would go smoothly. And everything did go smoothly. The stories began to accumulate, and they all seemed to be evidence of his presence rather than his absence.

That night, all of us were in the apartment, cell phones ringing, laughing and crying, my brothers dancing with my mother, drinking – we felt an incredible presence. Nothing was missing. Everything was there except his body. It felt as though our dad was celebrating with us. There was a presence of ecstasy, love, fullness, laughing and crying – kindness in how we were all relating to each other – the presence of soul.

The next day we all flew up to Pittsburgh. The grandchildren were there, my daughter brought candles, my son and nephews had stocked the refrigerator. They met us at the house, and were waiting for us there. My mother had forgotten the key to the house, and my sister had lost hers. Fifteen of us were standing there, waiting to get into the house – and there was only one key between us, my nephew had one.

So we go inside, and I go upstairs to my parents' bedroom. I was going to sleep with my mother, and I had to move a pile of my father's things to put my suitcase down. And under the pile was a small note on a yellow scrap of paper in my father's handwriting which said: "Make front door keys." Actually it said: "mk fr dr kys." I took the note to my mother and said: "Here's a note from dad." We all laughed and said "thank you, Poppy" – and then we went to the hardware store and made copies of the key. At 10 p.m., my brother and his wife showed up, so we took them into the kitchen to give them something to eat – and suddenly we heard a huge crash.

We jumped up and ran into the next room. There was shattered glass everywhere. A box of glass balls filled with water that my mother used for flower arrangements had mysteriously "exploded." And then we saw it: a very old bronze plaque, in bas relief, of my great-grandfather – my father's grandfather – was lying on the floor. My father had always referred to his grandfather as the true foundation rock of the family. The plaque had come crashing down and Isaac W. was lying on the floor, surrounded by broken glass and water everywhere. That plaque had been hanging on the wall for years, and I had never really looked at it. So we're all standing around looking at my great-grandfather on the floor, this person no one had ever paid any attention to except dad. My first thought was: "The ancestors are saying: Okay, we've got him now, he's in good hands." The next day, at the funeral home, my mom went to pick out the casket – my mom asked the director what time the body had arrived there. He said: "At ten thirty last night" – which was the exact time the plaque fell off the wall.

The next morning, my mother was going through my dad's closet, but she couldn't find an appropriate "formal" suit to dress my father in for the funeral. He had outgrown all his old business suits, and they had long since been given away. My mother is handing out his ties, and finally she sees his velour exercise jacket. We immediately knew that it was perfect. It was red, white and blue – and he was wearing a white shirt. So, for a lack of other clothes, he was dressed in red, white and blue – like the American flag. As I said, my dad was a supreme patriot. When I was younger, I had to come to peace with my father's "God bless America" stuff. He and I were at war in the 60's, our politics were so different. Much later, I came to realize that his patriotism, in his mind, was that all people, of all colors, of all creeds deserved the same opportunities. Anyway, he was dressed like a flag, and very comfortable.

At some point during our stay in Pittsburgh, I looked around and saw that we were all filled with the ideals that my father carried. The spirit, whatever his life stood for – each of us was carrying a different piece of it. My brothers, my sister, my children, my nephews, those ideals are embodied in us now. Everyone stepped into it, because it was the presence of spirit, and spirit is not separated from us by a physical body. That spirit became alive in us – not something "over there," separate and apart from us, in the physical form of my dad. His physical body was gone, but it was as if I could see little pieces of him, like small points of light in every one of us. We did not have to look for something outside ourselves to find my father. He was right here.

The Wind
from Eileen Maceri

On August 5, 1979, my 21-year old daughter Susan died in an auto-mobile accident, thousands of miles from us, while traveling cross-country with her husband and baby, who both survived without serious injury. They were returning from California, where her husband had recently been discharged from the Navy, and were on their way to live with us in New York state. The initial phone call informing us of the tragedy shocked and traumatized our family beyond what words could describe. We were plunged into a nightmare of having to face the ter-rible fact that we would never see her again. To spare me further pain, I was at first told she died instantly. But a phone call about two weeks later from a woman who said she had been with Susie during her last hours, as she lay by the side of the highway waiting for a helicopter ambulance to arrive at the desert area where the accident had occurred, revealed that she had suffered a great deal and had begged the woman to "tell my Mom I love her." On hearing this news, I began to experi-ence severe stabbing pains in the center of my chest, which, no matter how much I cried and released my emotions, nothing could relieve. Our whole family was in deep shock and mourning.

Shortly after the stranger's phone call, I had an extremely vivid experi-ence, which I later called a "dream," but which, deep in my heart, I believe really happened. In this "dream," it was night and I was in my bed, lying in my room, but not sleeping, when a light appeared in the corner by the door – a small bright light which expanded until it was lighting up the room. In this light Susie appeared, smiling and radiant-ly beautiful, dressed in white. She came over to my bed and sat down on the side of it, right next to me. I could feel the mattress actually pressing down under her weight. I sat up immediately, exclaiming with joy, "Susie! Is it really you?" It was such a real experience that whenev-er I speak of it, it is as if I am experiencing it again, and I can feel the happiness leaping up in my heart, just as it did then. I threw my arms around her and hugged her tightly. She hugged me, too, and it was wonderful just to hold her again! The warmth and firmness of her body next to mine felt so good, so strong, and I wanted to hold her close for-ever. We embraced for a long time – I didn't want to let her go – and she said, "Mom, I'm happy! You don't have to worry about me. I'm fine!" Then she stood up and, taking my hand, she gently pulled me up from my bed, saying, "Come with me, Mom." She led me down the hall to her bedroom, where her little boy, Jason, just 13-months old, was sleeping (He actually did sleep in this room at the time.) Leading me to his crib, she said, "Please take care of him for me." I assured her I would, and all of a sudden I found myself sitting upright in bed, wide awake. Susie was gone, and I was filled with wonder. Had it all been a dream or had it really happened? To this day, I'm not sure which dimension we were in, but I KNOW Susie made her way back to me, and that is what is important. After that visit, I still missed her, and continue to miss her today, but I was comforted beyond words to have had that moment with her, to hold her again, and to feel her warmth and love and assurance that she was happy.

My other daughters, Jeanie (age 20 at the time) and Linda (age 11 at the time), also had similar "real" dreams within a week or so of mine, in which they had visits from Susie, dressed in white just as I saw her, who told them essentially the same message, adding to each of them to

"please stop crying. I'm fine, but it holds me back
when you cry. I want you to know I'm happy."
To Jeanie she said, "We don't ever die.
Please tell others that. Our lives continue on,
so please don't cry anymore."

One more occurrence of this kind took place when, as he awakened from a nap in her room, Susie's father had a vision of her, standing a few feet away from him. He said she had on a white dress and was surrounded by light. Shocked and somewhat frightened, he hurriedly closed his eyes, rubbed them, and told himself it must be clothes draped over a chair or something that just looked like a person. As he opened his eyes again, he still saw Susie standing there, smiling down at him. This appearance unnerved him so much, he bolted from the room and came running to tell me about it.

The second death – that of my best friend, a man I had come to love deeply – occurred on July 4, 1982. Paul was a light in my life and in the life of my children. He seemed to carry sunshine around with him, and his dynamic energy uplifted all who knew him. When he walked into the room, it seemed to brighten and glow. He fully entered my life and my heart in 1980, and left my life – but not my heart – two short years later. During those too few months, we talked about life and death issues and covered every area of each other's lives with a deep passion to know as much about each other as we could. Looking back, it was almost as if we knew we would not have long in each other's company on this plane of existence so we wanted to pack in as much as we could. We laughed and cried together. He brought joy back into my life, and I will always be grateful to have had even two short years with him.

143

In the last week of June 1982, Paul called me excitedly one morning, exclaiming, "I have to tell you about the amazing thing that happened to me last night! I was lying on my bed; it was early evening, and I was not sleeping. All of a sudden, I felt a tug on my arm, and the tugging kept increasing. I started getting scared because it was beginning to hurt, when suddenly I popped out of my body! And there I was – standing by the bed, looking down at me still lying on the bed! It was incredible! I looked down at the body I was now in, and it was even better than the one on the bed – more muscular and everything!" (Paul worked out to keep his body in good shape, so this was important to him.)

He went on, exclaiming,
"I felt so light, and I could actually float!"
He continued to describe how he floated
through the walls of his home, and out
onto the lawn, strongly trying to
come and see me, but felt an
invisible barrier around his yard.

At that moment, he was pulled backwards so fast, he "thunked" back into his body on the bed. He was amazed and exhilarated at his experience and promised, "If it ever happens again, I'm going to try really hard to come and see you!"

I believe that out-of-body experience was given to Paul and me to prepare us for what was to come. Just one week later, on July 4, he was again "thunked" out of his body when a drunk driver suddenly swerved into his lane of traffic and hit him head-on. This time Paul was not to return to his physical body, as he died almost instantly.

The night after his death, as several of our friends and I sat in the living room of his home, all of us in shock and desperate sadness, suddenly the light beside my chair (where Paul always sat) began to blink on and off. Then a whooshing wind swept through the living room, blowing the drapes out from the windows and walls. But it was a still night and there were no windows open in the room! I knew immediately that it was Paul, letting us know he was all right. It was just like him to surprise us in such a dramatic way, and I could imagine him laughing at the looks on the faces of some of his macho friends, who stood up in fearful wonderment at what was occurring.

The next day, his friend Phil and I were standing in Paul's garage, talking about him and how much we missed him. I mentioned to Phil about some reading Paul and I had done about life after death and about how Paul came to believe in an afterlife in the years we were together. He also shared my interest in quantum physics' explanations that we live in a multi-dimensional universe. We did not understand the scientific depths of that science, but something deep within us both told us this was true. As we stood there in the garage, I told Phil about Paul's out-of-body experience. Then I mentioned the title of a book Paul and I had read, one that he claimed had changed his perceptions on life. At that very moment, I happened to glance down and, on the floor of the garage, right at our feet, was that very book – *The Seth Material* by Jane Roberts. Although we had been standing there for some time, we hadn't noticed it before. Wide-eyed, Phil and I looked at each other, as the realization arose of Paul's presence there with us. Picking up the book, I handed it to Phil, saying, "I think Paul wants you to read it." Phil, who had never been interested in spirituality, the supernatural, or anything except the material world, was very touched and vowed he would read the book.

Paul loved flowers and had some beautiful rose bushes in his garden. During our relationship, he often cut a white rose from one of the bushes and brought it to me, telling me it was a "rose grown just for you." Shortly after his death, I received a sympathy card from a friend.

> *On the front of the card was a picture*
> *of a white rose and the words,*
> *"A rose for you."*
> *Among other sympathetic sentiments,*
> *the verse said, "Love is eternal."*
> *As I read it, I felt like lightning was going*
> *through me. It seemed incredible, but I was*
> *certain the words were from Paul – his*
> *message to me was being sent in some*
> *wonderfully miraculous way*
> *through my friend.*

For several weeks right after his death – in my own home, at Paul's house, and even on a trip to a friend's home in Washington, D.C. – the light beside my chair or bed would flash rapidly on and off several times.

145

This happened every night while I was in Washington, and often when I was at home. My Washington friend assured me her lamp had never done that before. There was no discernible reason for these lamps to do that. They all had on/off switches that could not be toggled accidentally, and the wiring in each of them appeared to be in good order. I was sure it was Paul, and began to write letters to him in a notebook every night when I would go to bed. Soon I "heard" him – not his actual voice, but a feeling within me – talking to me. I started writing what I heard. They were beautiful letters telling me of his love and that eventually I would be joining him and we would continue our adventures together. Some might say it was just my imagination, but I really could feel him beside me, assuring me that everything was all right. After a while, I no longer wrote in the notebook, as it felt right to discontinue it and go on with my life. But over the years I have felt Paul near me frequently, sometimes in my car or beside me as I sit at a restaurant table – but mostly at night as I lie in bed. Up until about two years ago, the light on my dresser would occasionally blink on and off for no apparent reason. I always felt that was Paul telling me he still loved me. When I need help in any way, I think of Paul, who often promised me in life he would always be there for me, and I feel a reassurance that somehow he is still here beside me. I've noticed at these times that a cool breeze is wafting over me. It feels very calming and peaceful.

In the last few years, my father, my younger brother, and a dearly loved cousin have passed to the dimension beyond. And in March of this year my husband died. I believe they have all found that death is just a change of state, in which one enters a subtler dimension. I continue to read books on near-death experiences, and believe with all my being that these experiences are true.

Because of the love of Susie and Paul that reached out to assure me in my darkest moments, I am certain that life continues on in a finer realm, and I expect to see all my loved ones again when I cross into that world.

The Boat Ride
an Interview with Millie

Millie is a vibrant and loving Latino woman, who lives next door to us. I absolutely adore her. She grew up and lived in Brooklyn, and when she moved to Ithaca she brought with her three children, her furniture – and an entire culture. A framed painting of the Madonna hangs in her small downstairs hallway, and a cut-out picture of Christ and the Sacred Heart is taped on her refrigerator, just above a small photograph of her grandmother. A plain wooden cross hangs over her bed. And walking down the street, under her open windows, one hears Millie singing along to Salsa music playing on the radio, or happy or sad Latino songs – and one can also hear the excited, young voices of her children, who deeply love and respect her. If one climbs the painted stairs to visit her, she will most likely meet you at the top of the stairs, smiling and holding a broom or dustpan – or she is in the kitchen cooking up a storm of Spanish cuisine, which she then shares with half the neighborhood.

The other day I went over to Millie's house, to bring Christmas presents for the children. Marc Anthony was singing Spanish songs on the record player, and a Christmas tree was already set up and fully decorated in the living room – even though it was just after Thanksgiving. I was in a rush, and in my haste my jacket was half undone, my scarf was trailing the floor, one foot was sockless because the sock came off with my boot in the downstairs hallway and I did not want to take the time to put it back on – and I was precariously balancing a stack of wrapped presents between my arms. Millie took one look at me from the top of the stairs, laughed and said: "You look so cute. You look like you just ran away from home." She took me into the living room to show me the tree, and crossing the room said: "Come, see what Claudio gave me." It was a small plaster Christmas scene, with two old fashioned carolers, one on either side of the central thin, plaster tree. "It plays in Spanish," Millie said as she pressed a button, and on came a Christmas tune in Spanish, with a salsa beat. She had placed the music box on top of a light wooden cabinet with glass doors. "That's nice," I said nodding at the cabinet. "Is it new?" "I found it on the street," said Millie, and she gave me her wonderful, beautiful smile.

I could never place Millie between the covers of a single volume of pages – so I will not even try. I often tease her and say I will write a weekly TV show based on her life. (She asks: "What episode are we on now?" And I answer: "Episode 824." She says: "I thought we already did that episode.") Whenever I see her, something new and exciting, or tragic, or interesting in one of a thousand ways has happened to her. Millie breathes Life into life, and there is always good-hearted turmoil at her house. I remember the time I went to her youngest child's birthday party. Millie had just moved to Ithaca. She had bought matching plates, napkins and cups for the birthday celebration; candy and snacks waited in their bowls, plastic forks and spoons were set next to their plates, piles of homemade food bubbled and steamed on the stove. Only, Millie had forgotten to invite people to the party. Some events were more complicated and tragic – but as I say, there is always something new when you walk in Millie's front door.

Late one chilly autumn night, as I was reading in the living room, the phone rang. It was Millie. She had to go down to New York City because her grandmother was dying, would I come over and keep her company. I ran over to her house and up the painted stairs – to find her packing a small , worn suitcase and crying. She was trying to catch the next bus down to New York City, and she was packing her clothes, calling the bus station and various relatives and friends, and talking to me, all simultaneously. Between phone calls she said that her grandmother had taken care of her during her childhood, and she sobbed as she packed her few clothes and made arrangements for her children to be taken care of while she was away.

Some months later – it was now late summer – Millie came into my living room, sat down on the couch and said: "I can't stay long, but I have to tell you something." I asked what was wrong – her right leg was crudely bandaged from the knee down, and her dark eyes were unusually black and brilliant and reflecting some emotion that I could not yet identify. She launched into the following story, which she later retold for this interview:

Millie: Friends invited me onto their boat, and it was a beautiful day. We were eating fruits and just enjoying the sun on the water and I sat down on the side of the boat and then I fell into the lake.

I slipped off the boat and I went under the water. I couldn't come up. And suddenly I saw my grandmother there. While I was under the water, I saw her there.

Laurie: What did she look like?

M: She was wearing a pink dress and a pearl necklace – and she was smiling at me. It was so real. She looked so real.

She was right there. I could see her through the water. I wanted to go over to her and give her a hug.

She gave me the strength to come up from the water.

You know I can't swim – I panicked. I would have drowned because I panicked. Laurie, I thought I would die.

She gave me the strength to come up, and then my friends pulled me onto the boat. That's when I hurt my leg, when they pulled me up on the boat. I scraped my leg trying to climb the ladder.

I was seated on the chair in Millie's bedroom during this interview, writing what she said down on a piece of paper on my knee, while Millie wrapped birthday presents for her daughter Christina. Millie was sitting on the edge of her bed, surrounded by sprawling rolls of gaily-coloured patterned paper, half-unwound spools of ribbons and boxes and other presents in various stages of wrapping. Between sentences she sometimes stood up to pick out new wrapping paper for the next present, or to choose the perfect ribbon, or to relocate the ever-missing pair of plain metal scissors. And after retelling this story, and finishing her parental tasks – it was now well after midnight – Millie went into the kitchen and said, "That's how it was," turned on the light – and fixed me something to eat.

The Fluttering of Angels' Wings

an Interview with Gail

Gail: Cheryl Jean was my first cousin, and we were very close. I am the oldest grandchild, she is the third grandchild. This was on my mother's side of the family. I made her jello and pudding when she was a child, when I was earning my childcare badge for Girl Scouts. I spent weekends and vacations with her family at my grandmother's house. At fifteen she was a junior bridesmaid at my wedding.

She was a very pretty girl, angelic looking with blond hair and blue eyes. She died tragically at age twenty. She kissed her mother and said goodbye before she died. It was a car accident.

I did not go to her funeral service. I was living out of state, newly married, and really didn't have the financial means. I didn't get to go.

Laurie: But you had contact with her after she died?

G: It was about a year and a half or two years after her death. I was asleep. It was a very vivid experience and it feels like it happened yesterday. And I am retelling this at least twenty years later.

I had imagery that was not just visual, but also auditory. It was a whirling sound. As the apparition approached me, the sound was a whirling sound that became almost deafeningly loud. Almost like a helicopter.

The apparition included three beings – my cousin and two others who were with her. The presence of these beings was very gentle, they were not scary at all.

L: Do you think they were angels?

G: It felt like it was my cousin with two supportive beings that I thought were angel-like, yes. The two angels – I felt their wings. And because of the fluttering sounds, I thought it was the sound of their fluttering wings. That's why I thought it was two angels with my cousin.

And not only could I hear that my cousin was speaking to me, I could hear what she said.

L: What did she say?

G: First, she let me know that she was okay. Her being was around me, almost like a hug. She wanted me to know that she was happy and in a good place and okay. And then the whirling intensified. Then she asked if I wanted to go too. I briefly thought about it, whether I wanted to, and then I told her "No." And then they all moved on and I woke up.

L: *Did you have any other contact with her?*

G: I really haven't, but her sister has. My second experience of being contacted was recently, with my friend Sue. She died about a year and half ago. About a month after she died she contacted me. I was awake this time and I was sitting in my family room. I was by myself. I was looking out the patio room glass door, at the greenery of the bushes.

It seemed like we were separated by a low median wall, and she was on the other side of it. The strip between us was of a different color. To me it looked like a road or a path between us. It was like the median on the highway. She was just on the other side of it, and she was smiling and teasing me. She was dressed in her usual white, tailored LL Bean shirt. She was wearing her glasses, her haircut and hair color were the same – she looked exactly the same. She was smiling and waving at me and doing this crazy little song and dance routine, like vaudeville, da da da dum. She did it three times. Except, instead of doing the dance with her feet, she did it from the waist up and with her hand. I couldn't see her feet, I could only see her from the waist up because of the path or median strip between us. The other hand was down by her side.

L: *Did she make you laugh?*

G: It was very playful. It cheered me up and made me smile. It made me have this feeling that she was okay. It made me laugh – I wanted her to do it again.

Another instance of contact with another realm was with my in-laws, my husband's parents. We both would get the imagery of birds on important occasions in the family or in difficult times when we needed support.

L: *Could you explain?*

G: It happened many times. Birds, cardinals, have come to us at times you would not expect to see a cardinal. You would see the brightest red bird sitting in the tree in front of you. Sometimes the mate would come. This would happen when a child would ordinarily consult a parent for advice, during a difficult time. Or at a time when we would want them to share an experience, their grandchild's birthday, graduations, our

151

anniversary. It was their way of showing us that they were present. That happened five or ten times.

L: *Why cardinals, do you know?*

G: They loved cardinals. They both loved red, clothes, their kitchen – their house was red. They had a lamppost in the driveway next to their house and on the sign with the house number on it they had a metal cardinal. They had one in the coleus, a wooden, spinning cardinal, the tail moved.

Another contact with someone in another realm was with my grandparents on my father's side of the family – in the imagery of a clock.

L: *Could you explain?*

G: My grandparents' house was number 530 Elm Street. The first time they contacted me was at 5:30 in the afternoon.

L: *What do you mean by "contact"?*

G: I felt the presence of both of them, and they were giving me information. It was a supportive thing. I was feeling alone and sad, and it was a feeling of supportive energy, a feeling of love. The first time they just let me know that they were there. They were in another realm, I was in the kitchen, and I just knew that the realm they were in wasn't very far away but I couldn't see them. They let me know that 5:30 would be a time I could contact them in the future.

There are times when I am not consciously trying to contact them at 5:30, but they're there again. It happens in the kitchen and in the car. This has happened fifteen to twenty times. My husband has also had contact with them at that time.

L. *Thank you for this interview, dear Gail.*

Out-of-Body Dreams
an Interview with JB

JB is one of the more sane and most honest people I have ever known. In fact, I especially love her way of self-reflecting and poking fun at herself when she's made a mistake or failed to meet her own expectations. She has always struck me as a most interesting combination of depth of feeling and a grand sense of humor, and I always welcome our interactions. So in reading the following interview be sure to hear some wonderful laughter here and there.

Laurie: Tell us something about your "out-of-body" experiences.

JB: Well, I'd be asleep, or falling asleep and I'd begin to hear a rushing sound in my ears, like being next to a waterfall. In my mind, I was awake, and I'd try to move and I couldn't move. I didn't know that I could leave my body. I'd be lying on my bed paralyzed and I couldn't talk. It was scary, so I'd try to break out of it, get out of it. So I'd put all my concentration on my pinkie and say to myself, "Lift your pinkie, lift your pinkie." Once I could move my little finger, the rushing sound would subside and I would be here again, on this level.

L: Once you were able to move your little finger you would break out of the paralysis and again be in this familiar waking state reality?

JB: Yes. If I could move my pinkie, it was like a mirror shattering in silence. All of a sudden the sensation of rushing in my ears stopped and I could move. I was back in my bed.

It's hard to put it into words, to describe it. I think the paralysis is an important part of it. The body is paralyzed so that I'm not able to distract myself from this other state of being. Because if I break myself out of the paralysis, I'm back in the familiar consciousness.

L: Are you awake, are you fully conscious during your out-of-body experiences?

JB: I think I am awake because when I stay in there, in that state – I am aware of the room around me, the bed, I can feel the air as I move through it, I can see other people – and it all looks and feels the same as it usually does.

L: It looks the same as it does in waking state reality?

JB: Yes.

L: What is different?

JB: I float in the air. And I've been able to do somersaults in the air. After this experience happened a number of times, when I was living in Ithaca, I started doing somersaults above the bed. I go way above my bed so that I can tuck in and do a somersault – like one does in the water. When I'm in the body, I'm bound by gravity.

I would also go to other rooms in the house. I would fly to the other rooms, I was suspended in the air. At one point I remember looking down at myself sleeping on the bed.

L: How did you feel when you looked down and saw yourself still asleep on the bed?

JB: I never got rid of the fear. At first I thought I was dying and that I wouldn't be able to get back into my body. But after a while I realized that I could get back. And then I wasn't so desperate to move my pinkie, to break out of it.

L: Make your finger move in order to stop the out-of-body experience?

JB: Yes.

L: What did you see when you were out of your body?

JB: Everything looked the same as in this reality. It was darker because it was nighttime. There wasn't much to see, everyone else was asleep in their beds.

L: In other words, if your mom – in our shared waking state reality – had been in the kitchen at 11pm, in your out-of-body state you could have floated into the kitchen, looked at the clock and the clock would have said 11pm. And you would have seen your mom baking cookies. And you could have watched her put them in the oven?

JB: Yes.

L: Or if you had decided, on New Years Eve, to visit Times Square, you could have traveled there in this state of consciousness and seen the crowds and the ball dropping at midnight?

JB: Yes.

L: In other words, in these experiences you are seeing the world as it actually is in waking state reality. You are not in a personal reality, such as in dream state?

JB: Yes. I am seeing the world as it actually is.

L: I myself have never had an out-of-body experience such as yours. But I have read of them. In my readings, people have traveled all over the world while in this state of consciousness, in this subtle body. Did you ever try to leave your house?

JB: When I lived in the attic room on Quarry Street, I went out the window and came right back in because I was really scared. It was a garret, and there was a tiny window next to a big square chimney in the middle of this tiny garret room. I said to myself: "Let me try this, I'll hang in for this one" – and I went out the window. It was a tiny square window. But I was too scared, so I came right back in.

I think it's interesting that it hasn't happened for many, many years. Sometimes I miss it. And it's not something I can make happen.

L: Why were you given this ability do you think, what did you learn from it?

JB: Well, I think the biggest thing I learned was that the physical world that we perceive with our five senses isn't everything. That however compelling it may be and is, the world around us, the books in the bookshelf, family, friends, those who make up our world – all of that isn't everything.

When I had these experiences, I was too young and too scared to really understand the profound nature of the gift. I was, at that time in my life, very much dependent on the books in the bookshelf and the friends around me. I didn't have the means or the courage to acknowledge that there was something more important and it was being handed to me. The gift to be able to experience something other than the physical world.

L: It seems to also prove that we are more than just the physical body. It is an astounding concept, that we can experience the world and its happenings with crystal-clear awareness while our physical body is left behind, asleep on our bed. That our Consciousness, our essence, is not tethered to the physical body. As a clairvoyant, I experience this all the time. And I also can travel all over the world, see what is going on in other places on our Earth, or even beyond our Earth. But I have never been aware of a subtle body such as the one you are given in these out-of-body experiences. Nor have I ever, during my experiences, seen my material, physical body where it is on Earth during my experiences. It is as though we are between Heaven and Earth at these times, and that these experiences can bring us closer to Heaven. Thank you for this interview. If this experience is given to you in the future, I hope that you will be able to enjoy the adventure and the freedom it brings. And perhaps even learn interesting things during your various investigations, while in your out-of-body state.

JB: I hope it does come back. I think as I age, am around longer and longer, I am learning not to be afraid of this life or of dying. Because I was so terrified of dying, I was afraid of the experience. I think I am learning that leaving the body in this way isn't the same thing as dying. Probably a great deal is to be gained by going through with the experience.

L: What if I said the experience was almost exactly the same as dying. That when we so-called "die," we leave the physical body behind and our consciousness continues and we are fine. Just as in your out-of-body experiences.

JB: I am getting closer to accepting that.

Laurie: Julie is your daughter?

Sidney: Yes. Julie was eighteen in October, and she was just on her way to work and the weather was really bad. The snow was coming down, huge flakes. Before she left for work, I opened the front door and said to her: "Come and check this out. It's so beautiful." And it was. Later, I was in the living room, and suddenly I came flying off the couch and looked at the clock.

Julie was going to call me when she got to work. At that point she wouldn't have been late for work, it was somewhere after noon, and she didn't have to be there until 12:30. So I called her cell phone and got the message, her voice mail.

Then I called her work, to see if they had heard from her, and they had not. I was starting to become frantic, because I could tell that something was really wrong. So I ended up calling the sheriff's office, because the weather was so bad. I was afraid she had gone off the hill. It is enormous and steep, and if she went off it, no one would know. So I called the sheriff's office and asked them to check it. They told me that no accident had been reported. I convinced them to check the hill, and they said they would.

So then I remembered that she was going to the post office first. I called them. She had already picked up the mail.

All of a sudden I'm starting to hear: "You need to get dressed," because I was still in my pajamas. So I went upstairs and got dressed and carried my shoes – I heard that I didn't need to put them on yet. And then I hear: "You need to take your blood pressure medication, you're going to really need it." So I took my blood pressure medication as instructed, and I went to put on some makeup and I hear: "You don't need to worry about the mascara." So I didn't put on any mascara.

L: Do you usually wear mascara?

S: I always wear mascara.

L: Do you think that Julie, or whatever being was speaking to you, was saying "Don't put on mascara, it will only make a big mess when you get the news and start to cry?"

157

S: I know that's why I was told not to bother putting it on.

L: *When you say: "Then I heard," what exactly do you mean?*

S: I don't know if you would call it thoughts. These thoughts were there, like usual thoughts – but the thoughts were not mine.

L: *So you heard them inwardly.*

S: Yes.

L: *Did a sense of peace come with them?*

S: After I spoke to the post office, when I heard the words "You need to get dressed," the frantic, absolute terror seemed to subside. And then I hear: "You need to go feed the crows." And I'm thinking "I can't go feed the crows, I need to be here to hear the phone." So I didn't immediately go outside to feed the crows. Normally I feed the crows when I feed the horse, but I had forgotten to take the food out for the crows. I called Julie's work again, to see if they had heard from her, and they had not.

I listened to the phone machine messages, and a very dear friend of hers – a young man who had been very dear to her – had left a message for her. He had been away at Marine boot camp for two months. They hadn't spoken in all that time, but that morning he had called her.

So I got my crow bucket, put on my farmer gear, and went to feed the crows. I put the food out for them. I have a big medicine wheel there.

L: *What is a medicine wheel?*

S: A medicine wheel is in the form of a circle. The Native Americans believed that there is Power in each direction, such as East, West, North and South. They pray and direct prayers to the Spirit Keepers of the four directions. They also include Mother Earth and Father Sky, making it actually six directions. And by praying and acknowledging each direction, you invite in the Powers of the Universe.

L: *Where are you from?*

S: Kentucky. I guess you're wondering about my Southern drawl?

L: *I couldn't begin to get it down on paper.*

S: So that morning I went to my wheel – actually it's the concrete base of an old corn crib. And I stood in the center and prayed to each direction. That she'd be safe. I finished praying and gathered up my bucket, and was heading back to the house when the state troopers came in the driveway. They're getting out of the truck and coming up the drive. One guy introduced them both, I don't remember their names. And he says: "There's been an accident over on 34B." And I go: "And?" And he says: "Your daughter Julie was involved and she didn't make it."

L: What did you do?

S: I think I said, "I knew it." One of them was a woman, and she said, "Oh, that's right, you called." Then it was to get into the house. I was on my knees in the driveway.

The world changed. It was the world before, and now it is the world after.

I don't remember where I was when I had the first contact with Julie after the event, but she said to me, "Mama, I am safe."

L: That's what you prayed for.

S: Yes. I hadn't prayed that she be alive. I prayed that she would be safe.

L: Did you, at this time, hear her voice instead of your own?

S: Yes.

L: So it sounded like her voice.

S: Yes.

L: At that time, did you feel a presence of love and peace, when she was speaking to you?

S: No. I was so overwrought and distraught. People have asked me how this feels. And the best way I can describe it – and I guess it's my Kentucky roots – is that it's like going feet first into a meat grinder.

L: So at that time, the message didn't really help.

S: There was peace. There was peace around that period of time. But I was grieving so completely. At some point during the next couple of days, I was cryin' and I could feel myself being pulled into a hole – a big, dark, deep place.

159

L: *Did Julie contact you again?*

S: The next time that I had any kind of contact – I'm thinkin' that it must have been two weeks later, I'm not real sure... The living room was Julie's room to clean, we each had a room to clean. And it was always a fight, to get her to clean that room. And I was cleaning it for the first time since the accident. It took me all day. And there was a point during the afternoon, I was carrying something up to my room, and I laid face down on the bed and cried. I felt pressure on my legs, a physical pressure. This was not something I was imagining. The pressure went up my legs and across my back – as though she were lying over me, on me, in me, a part of me. My eyes were closed, I was sort of covering my head with my arms. And I remember seeing – I guess the best way to describe it is a pulsating essence of Light. There was a nucleus of sorts that was moving. And there were these spokes of Light that radiated out from that nucleus, and in between those were other spokes of Light. And Julie's face, her earthly face, kept fading in and out of the nucleus. The whole thing was Light and moving. It was the essence of Julie, a twinkling, a fireball. I said: "You look so beautiful. You look like a snowflake." Because that's what it reminded me of, a snowflake.

L: *So when you say the essence was made of Light, was it a sort we might find here on Earth?*

S: No. It was almost a mist in Light. A cloud, a fog, a mist. It was alive.

L: *Were there sparkles in this mist of Light?*

S: Yes. Twinkles.

L: *I'll tell you why I am asking this. When I was in my late twenties, a friend of mine left for other realms. And one day, maybe a few weeks later, while I was on my bed, a cloud appeared near the bed. It too was like a mist, a quickly vibrating mist of sorts, made up of many moving bits of brilliant, twirling, sparkling Light. It remained hanging there for some minutes, and then disappeared. A friend came into my room about ten minutes later and said, "What's all this vapor in here?" My friend was looking at the remnants of the cloud, and put his hand up, to feel the vapor.*

S: Oh my.

L: *I was going to include it in the story about Daniel that I wrote for this book, but decided against it. Interesting, a few nights ago I again asked myself if I should include it in his story, and almost did. Maybe now I will. Did the cloud you saw have bright coloured sparkles here and there?*

S: I don't remember seeing any.

L: That's probably because my friend Daniel killed himself. The coloured sparkles I saw were probably his deep grief and other emotions. His anger and his grief, his regret. Did you hear a voice?

S: Nope. No speaking. I spoke to her. I remember holding her.

L: Was it a distance away from you? Mine was in the center of the room.

S: No. I was still lying down on the bed, with my eyes shut. I'm seeing her in my mind, it's almost as if the back of my eyelids is the screen. That's where the image is projected. And because that's where it is, I could put my hands across my own face, and I felt as if I was holding her. That's exactly what it felt like. As much as I wanted to stay there with her, I couldn't. And I knew I couldn't.

L: Did you just fall asleep?

S: No. I withdrew. It was a willing, a knowing withdrawal. If that makes any sense.

L: Have you had any other experiences of this sort?

S: Yes. I'd been having a really rough time. I could not stop crying. I couldn't pull myself out of the grief. It's like standing at the edge of the ocean, and you're getting bombarded by the waves. Some of them are big, some of them are not so big, and some of them bring you to your knees. You just feel as though you are drowning in the grief.

There are pictures of Julie all over the house, even before the world changed there were pictures of her all over the house. Every time I passed one of her pictures I'd say, "I love you baby girl." And this had been goin' on for at least a week. Then I got a phone call from one of Julie's friends. The friend said that she's had a dream, and that she had talked to Julie. And Julie had a message for me. The message for me was that she was really all right and that she loved her hair. When I heard it I had to laugh. Julie really hated her hair. She had beautiful hair, and enough on her head for four people. It was nice and wavy like mine, and twice as thick. She would wear it tight against her head, in a bun. She said it was too "poofy." She had so much hair that when she washed it in the shower, she'd just stick the hair that fell out on the wall of the shower – she was afraid it would clog the drain. I fussed at her about it.

161

So I was in the shower, and I look over, and there's a hair on the wall – in the shape of a heart. This is after a week of me saying, "I love you baby girl." It was like an "I love you" to mama. And it stayed upon the wall long enough for me to show my son.

The next thing that happened (this was a good two months into this) and I had not painted or sketched or done anything artistic at all. For some reason, I do not know why, I went into my studio. I have a DVD of Josh Groban, I put that on the TV and I sat down on my couch and started to draw.

I have crystals hanging in the windows of my studio. And when the sun hits them, of course, they reflect prisms all over the place. Now, the doors are shut. The doors are louvre doors, with half louvre on the bottom and the top is a frosted glass. No one has been in or out of the studio, the louvre doors have not been opened. All the windows are closed shut, and there's very little draft because the windows are new and sealed. It's about two or three in the afternoon, so the sun is in the west. I just happened to look up at the prisms that were reflecting on the louvre door, and there are two prisms, one that is probably about twelve inches higher than the other one.

And they begin to move. Gently at first, and then the swing got bigger and bigger – to the point where the reflection of the prisms was swinging over the width of two doors. And I hear her say to me, in her own voice: "Dance with me, Mommy." And that's significant in that since they were very little children, both my children and I have danced together in the kitchen. One first and then the other. "My turn," "My turn…"

It's been probably two or three weeks now that I've been seeing lights.

L: Lights? What do they do?

S: The best way I can describe them – it's like being behind a shooting star. It's like looking at a shooting star from behind. And it moves, these lights flash. It's bigger as it takes off, just like a ball of light with a trail, a tail behind it. Very, very bright. Not all consuming.

L: Are your eyes open – or shut?

S: Open and shut, I see them both ways. But they are brighter and clearer with my eyes open. And they are different sizes. The night before last, I stood at the doorway to her room. I was saying to her, in my mind: "If these lights, if this is you, give me a sign." And within a few moments, one of the lights went right up my right eye, and three smaller ones danced across my left eye.

L: *How frequent are these lights?*

S: Probably not more than twice a day. But some of them have been so bright it's almost as though there is movement in the room, because I turn my head to look.

L: *So, in other words, they are outside of you, in the room?*

S: Yes. This is definitely outside of me.

L: *Have you felt a presence of love?*

S: Yes. The incredible love that I have felt for this child lives on. Her crossing over has taken her physical presence, but the enormous love continues to grow in my heart.

L: *Do you feel love from her?*

S: Yes. Watching those prisms dance – I could feel her loving me. And that went on for quite a while.

L: *Would you say you felt a presence of love surrounding you at those times?*

S: I would say that it filled the room.

L: *Does this happen with the flashes of light?*

S: It did when I asked for a sign and when I received it. And it made me smile so big.

L: *Because you were happy?*

S: No, because it again confirms what I know to be true. I still have a relationship with her. It's just different. I know she has a far greater capacity to love and protect others than while she was still on Earth. I have not lost her. It was not her big brown eyes and her beautiful, long hair – that was not what I loved so. I loved her essence, and I continue to love it. And I love it even more than I did before.

L: *This book is to give people hope.*

S: That's why I am here tonight. If one person reads this and it opens the mind to the possibility of contact with spirit, with the spirit of a loved one – then it is worth reliving this tragedy. Spirits whisper, they don't yell. And if you are consumed with grief, you can't hear it. I find

163

that when I am wallowing in the grief of it, I can't hear it.

L: The spirit?

S: Yes. Specifically Julie. I would have missed those beautiful dangling prisms as they swung back and forth across the louvre doors. It's a waste of time to keep saying "This didn't happen." I must have said it a hundred times. And then I realized that the task was to build a life that includes her, but in a different way.

L: Thank you for this interview.

S: It was nice to meet you.

 ## The Voice
an Interview with Cynthia

This dream is not an example of astral travel, or of going to other realms. But in this Dream Cynthia found what we are all looking for, what we are all seeking while on this Earth.[34]

Cynthia is an artist, a painter who lives next to us at Windgarth, our lake house. I always think of Cynthia among her many gardens, sur-rounded by mounds of cuttings and various garden tools, her wooden pushcart nearby, primed to fix some patch or in the midst of creating a new space for a new plant, moving with a certain economy of movement, stillness and grace – sometimes working by flashlight in her back garden well into the night. At those times she looks more like a young woman in her early twenties than a woman in her golden years.

Some nights we stand on the dock, or in the middle of our narrow front road, and watch the moon reflected off the lake in a band of pure light reaching to our feet, or half hidden by clouds over the fields and vine-yards across the road. And on sunny summer days we often sit on her dock and talk or eat some watermelon she has brought down from the house or some other treat she has made or bought, and watch the colours of the water around us change in hue and intensity as the clouds run across the sky. One afternoon, while I was scribbling in my notebook, she told me the following story:

Cynthia: I never understood the words in the Bible "In order to know God you have to give up yourself," or something like that, I'm not sure of the words. I never knew what that meant. How do you give up your-self? But then there was a time in my life when I was alienated from my daughter, my husband left me – it was a terrible time. And one night I said, "Please Lord, take over," before I went to sleep. And that night I had a dream.

And in my sleep, I saw Him. Not a person, but just a bright, warm Light. He, I think it was God, told me that I had to do something; I had to find a person I knew and tell him that I forgave him. He wasn't living in the area any more. I called everyone I knew about him. I tried for years to get a hold of this man.

My whole world changed after this dream. The world is wonderful. We

---

[34] *My dear friend Cynthia died in a fatal car crash a few short months after this interview.*

don't know it, but the world is a fantastic place and life is beautiful. Everything was suddenly so calm, so perfect, so happy. And I felt so protected.

Laurie: How do you know this wasn't just an ordinary dream?

C: Because my whole life changed.

Years later my son died in a biking accident. I was praying and crying all the way to the hospital, I was fighting it and repeating, "Please let him be alive" – and then all of a sudden I found myself saying, "Thank you Lord for taking care of me." Since then – He's there all the time, a warm space that's always there. I see His presence every day, in little ways.

Photos

Laurie Conrad

Laurie's Father & Grandmother

Laurie writing *Realms of Light*
at Windgarth. Sheldrake, New York

Eleanor

Ramana & Samantha

Louise McConnell

Jude & her grandchild Emily

Elisabeth

JF

Linda Ruth

JB

MG

Mabel

Diana Souza

Cynthia

Betty Joan

Jeremy

Jeremy's mother Betty

Meryl (3rd from right) & her son Conor
(front, 2nd from right) & their family

Millie

Sidney & Julie

Inger

Cindy

Angela

Igor (R) & Sergei (L)

JF's cats (L–R) Karima, Julie & Princess

Postludes

Dealing with Grief

As a clairvoyant, I can see my loved ones in other realms. I feel Louise take my arm often and hear her laughing. This doesn't mean that I would not want her to actually walk into the room, embodied. It is a different sort of hug from realm to realm, a bit more intangible. Even for the clairvoyant, the physical loss is not always an easy one – although over time we become familiar with the changes in form, the new reality. The Beauty of it. In some ways it is more Beautiful – the transparency and the clarity are breathtaking, the simplicity of feeling. It becomes a different relationship, and in many ways it is deeper, stronger and more tender than ever. And the Love is so immense and continuous, on all sides. No disputes, no disagreements. No egos to deal with. Just the Love.

Do I still miss them all, in their physical bodies? Yes! Do I still cry sometimes? Yes! But it is a different sort of missing them – because they are here with me. So I am crying a little while they themselves comfort me. And after I cry a little, then I can just enjoy our relationship the way it is, with all the differences in realms and forms. Our realms are not that different, nor that distant; the body I carry with me does not fully obscure the soul. There is a constant interweaving of Hearts, both here on Earth and from realm to realm, that most of us are not consciously aware of. That does not mean that this connection does not exist. It is only hidden from us.

For the non-clairvoyant, more Faith is needed. And when one develops that Faith, then one begins to feel the Love coming from those realms. Then we have the comfort and support of that Love.

The beings in other realms Love us with a Love we can barely imagine – and they wish us to know this. Our grief can block the Love they send us. So this Faith is important for the Peace and flow of Love from realm to realm, for and from all beings, in all realms.

On Earth we experience a separation that is not ultimately real. Once we reach a certain level of spiritual attainment, those separations begin to dissolve. Ultimately – we are all the same essence, and every relationship is soul to soul. The dog, the cat, my mother, my neighbor, my friend, the saint – we are all one and indistinguishable in Source and Essence. The individual forms are just

167

floating n that Divine Essence. That is what I clairvoyantly see. Even the coal stove is a form floating on that Divinity. Clairvoyantly, what I see is so wondrous. My clairvoyance is not limited to: "Your father just showed up in my living room." What I see is immense, infinitely complicated and infinitely simple. The wonder and the beauty of what I am sometimes shown, what we are actually living, could not be put into words. What we humans normally experience and perceive – is only the tip of the iceberg. I am now struggling to express the wonder that I feel and the magic of the interweavings of realities that exist in our lives – and the Divine Ideas behind the realities. So immense, and all so carefully orchestrated. Sometimes, if we get even a glimpse, we will call it mere coincidence – if we even notice.

What I clairvoyantly see is that we are all connected, human heart to human heart and hearts from realm to realm.

What I clairvoyantly glimpse is very like the motives and musical themes, phrases and sections of a beautiful piece that I am composing or interpreting on the piano. Themes and tones come into being, creating musical lines and harmonies, so many layers effortlessly forming to create this one moment in time. All the words in any book I could write might create a second of experience in our lives. Even the most advanced and mystical clairvoyants only get a brief Glimpse of this intricate truth.

Why all this is kept from us here on Earth is a mystery. If we saw this beautiful immensity and intricacy, we would be so grateful, and we would live entirely different lives.

Using what words I can find, I am trying to present the concept, the idea that this immense and complicated larger Reality exists. That we do not know, do not see the entire picture. Because if we think this conventional, physical Earth reality is all there is – then we are headed for a lot of trouble and much suffering. If I am experiencing a difficult time, I tell myself that I am not seeing the entire picture, I will undoubtedly never know the whole picture. But I do know that Divine Ideas are at work, every moment of every day, and that Divine Love is behind every event in the universe. Either the Divine has caused the event or the Divine allowed it for the good of the souls involved. Knowing that I do not know everything, that I do not see the whole – brings me back to Peace.

As for the natural and understandable pain of loss that you are feeling: with practice, the knowledge that we are the soul becomes abiding. At that point, one stands in that knowledge while experiencing the pain of the moment. The pain then becomes like a cloud briefly passing before the sun, the blue sky only temporarily and partially obscured. In our daily lives we are aware of both – the pain and suffering and disappointments of life and the remembrance that we are the Soul.

In my experience, the only true antidote to the suffering of life is to remember that we are all the Eternal Soul.

By the Lake

A lone sailboat
makes its way across the lake,
and its wake leaves a white trail
on the blue water.
And then the silence,
save for the wind and the crickets.

We are like the boat,
trailing our personal history.
And the silence
and the wind and the crickets —
are the Soul.

The soul's silence and Light and Love
are eternal and all-pervasive,
a perfect reflection of the Divine.

We live and travel in many realms,
not just this earthly one.
Whether we do so consciously or not,
we visit many Lakes in many realms,
and ride in many boats
and leave many trails of foam
and brightness behind us.

And all these experiences
are imprinted upon the soul,
in our deepest memory.

True Life and the Soul
are far more Infinite —
than we could ever imagine.

EPILOGUE

If I inwardly ask if a person – or any creature – is "alive" or "dead," I always clairvoyantly "get" that the person is alive. The answer is always the same. The being is always alive.

When people call me for Healing or to locate a lost person or animal, in the clairvoyant movie in my mind, I sometimes see the person or animal and where they are. However, I cannot determine whether they are "alive" or "dead." They always look the same to me clairvoyantly, no matter what realm they are in. I believe that this is true for all clairvoyants. There is no "alive" or "dead," clairvoyantly. For myself, this is perhaps the most profound proof that we never "die," and that the soul is eternal.

My friend and singer Louise has a presence so strong from other realms, that her little grandchild said Louise felt as real as the couch she was sitting on. Many non-clairvoyants in this volume have said that they too feel a strong presence of love and peace from their loved ones who are now in other realms. And they are universally perceived as almost transparent beings of Light, still in their earthly forms, young and beautiful and radiant – full of Peace and Joy. Their messages are ones of love and comfort. Or just a friendly "hello" as with my dear friend Joan.

Many of us have met our loved ones who are now in other realms, in dreams – in special dreams, vivid dreams that are true meetings either

here or in other realms. And afterwards, the memory of these meetings or "dreams" does not fade nor need to be written down – we do not forget them: they are permanently etched in our minds and hearts and souls. And when we look back, even many years later – we know that these experiences were true.

I hope that this volume has addressed the questions and fears of my friend Linda, as outlined in the Introduction. Certainly the stories in this book say that we do not "die," that we are not just "lumps in the ground" when this life on Earth is over. And that soul to soul communication continues, no matter what realm we are in. I have tried to share what I see and experience of other realms, and have interviewed others and carefully written down their stories. I feel that there is often a striking similarity to our experiences – and predictable reactions to those experiences.

The messages received from people in this book, from those they love in other realms, also seem to have a common thread: Pray for us. Love each other and take care of each other. Keep the family together. And last but not least: I love you. Whether we are in the body or not, in separate realms or in the same realm – I will love you always. Our Love is eternal.

Peace to those who read these lines.

For more information about clairvoyant experiences of life after death, there is an additional chapter of "Frequently Asked Questions" available online at the author's website:

Figaro Books
www.figarobooks.com

Go to the Community section, then to A Mystic's Journal.

. . . . .

Read all about the book's visual development and design strategies at the designer's website:

View from a Canary Perch
www.canaryperch.com

*Go to the Coal Mine section, then to Diana Souza's
article "A Designer's Journal."*

also by Laurie Conrad

The Spiritual Life of Animals & Plants

"These are touching stories, written by an extraordinary person."

Katy Payne, **author**
Silent Thunder: In the Presence of Elephants

"Have you ever had such a close relationship with a pet that you felt you could read their thoughts and know their feelings? Well, in the book **The Spiritual Life of Animals and Plants**, *Laurie Conrad shares her enlightening stories and tales of the animals and plants in her life and the communications she has shared with them. An uplifting collection of stories, sure to bring a smile to your heart."*

New Age Journal

"If you've ever wondered if animals and plants have souls, then you will love reading Laurie Conrad's **The Spiritual Life of Animals and Plants**. *Through the eyes and ears of a composer and musician, Conrad weaves wonderful little tales about the plants and animals that she has come to know and love in her life. By the time I had completed reading Laurie Conrad's book, I felt grounded in the knowledge that plants and animals do indeed lead spiritual lives and that as caretakers of our Earth, we humans have an obligation to live more consciously of all the soulful creatures who exist within this realm."*

Jeni Mayer, **Body Mind Spirit magazine**

"What a unique collection of stories! **The Spiritual Life of Animals and Plants** *gave me a whole new perspective on the animal (and even insect) beings who so closely share the Earth with us. If you'd like to expand your 'circle of compassion,' read this book."*

Carol Kline, *co-author*
Chicken Soup for the Pet Lover's Soul
Chicken Soup for the Cat & Dog Lover's Soul

LaVergne, TN USA
21 March 2010
176691LV00005B/74/P